1999 Supplement
CASES AND MATERIALS ON
EMPLOYMENT DISCRIMINATION

1999 Supplement

CASES AND MATERIALS ON EMPLOYMENT DISCRIMINATION

Fourth Edition

MICHAEL J. ZIMMER

Professor of Law
Seton Hall University

CHARLES A. SULLIVAN

Professor of Law
Seton Hall University

RICHARD F. RICHARDS

Professor of Law
University of Arkansas, Fayetteville

DEBORAH A. CALLOWAY

Professor of Law
University of Connecticut

ASPEN LAW & BUSINESS
A Division of Aspen Publishers, Inc.
Gaithersburg   New York

About Aspen Law & Business
Legal Education Division

In 1996, Aspen Law & Business welcomed the Law School Division of Little, Brown and Company into its growing business — already established as a leading provider of practical information to legal practitioners.

Acquiring much more than a prestigious collection of educational publications by the country's foremost authors, Aspen Law & Business inherited the long-standing Little, Brown tradition of excellence — born over 150 years ago. As one of America's oldest and most venerable publishing houses, Little, Brown and Company commenced in a world of change and challenge, innovation and growth. Sharing that same spirit, Aspen Law & Business has dedicated itself to continuing and strengthening the integrity begun so many years ago.

ASPEN LAW & BUSINESS
A Division of Aspen Publishers, Inc.
A Wolters Kluwer Company

CONTENTS

PART I

THE EMPLOYMENT RELATION AND
THE PROBLEM OF DISCRIMINATION

Chapter 2

The Policy Bases for Antidiscrimination Law

PART II

THE CONCEPT OF DISCRIMINATION
UNDER TITLE VII, THE AGE DISCRIMINATION
IN EMPLOYMENT ACT, AND SECTION 1981

Chapter 3

Individual Disparate Treatment Discrimination

Chapter 4

Systemic Disparate Treatment Discrimination   27

Chapter 5

Systemic Disparate Impact Discrimination   33

Chapter 6

The Interrelation of the Disparate Treatment
and Disparate Impact Theories of Discrimination   39

Chapter 7

Special Problems in Applying Title VII,
Section 1981, and the ADEA   43

Contents

PART III

ALTERNATIVE APPROACHES TO DISCRIMINATION

Chapter 8

Disability Discrimination

PART IV

PROCEDURES AND REMEDIES   149

Chapter 10

Procedures for Enforcing Antidiscrimination Laws   151

Chapter 11

Judicial Relief   165

TABLE OF CASES

TABLE OF SELECTED
SECONDARY AUTHORITIES

References are to Casebook page numbers.

Articles

Abrams, Douglas E., Arbitrability in Recent Federal Civil Rights Legislation: The Need for Amendment, 26 Conn. L. Rev. 521 (1994), 1112

Araujo, Robert John, "The Harvest Is Plentiful, but The Laborers Are Few": Hiring Practices and Religiously Affiliated Universities, 30 U. Rich. L. Rev. 713 (1996), 749

Ayres, Ian & Peter Siegelman, The Q-Word as Red Herring: Why Disparate Impact Liability Does Not Induce Hiring Quotas, 74 Tex. L. Rev. 1487 (1996), 417

Ayres, Ian & Frederick E. Vars, When Does Private Discrimination Justify Public Affirmative Action?, 98 Colum. L. Rev. 1577 (1998), 396

Bartlett, Katherine T., Only Girls Wear Barrettes: Dress and Appearance Standards, Community Norms, and Workplace Equality, 92 Mich. L. Rev. 2541 (1994), 695

Beiner, Theresa M. & John M.A. DiPappa, Hostile Environments and the Religious Employee, 19 U. Ark. Little Rock L.J. 577 (1997), 726

Beiner, Theresa M., Do Reindeer Games Count as Terms, Conditions or Privileges of Employment Under Title VII?, 37 B.C. L. Rev. 643 (1996), 127

Bingham, Lisa B., On Repeat Players, Adhesive Contracts, and the Use of Statistics in Judicial Review of Employment Arbitration Awards, 29 McGeorge L. Rev. 223 (1998), 1112

Bisom-Rapp, Susan, Bullet-Proofing the Workplace: Symbol and Substance in Employment Discrimination Law Practice, 26 Fla. St. U. L. Rev. ___, ___ (1999), 157

ACKNOWLEDGMENTS

The authors would like to thank the following members of the Seton Hall Class of 2000 for their untiring, if not uncomplaining, research assistance in the preparation of this Supplement:

Richard Kielbania
Chantal Kopp
Shannon Philpott

This Supplement incorporates the material found in the 1998 Professor's Update and adds developments current to January 1, 1999.

MJZ
CAS
RFR
DAC

PART I

THE EMPLOYMENT RELATION AND THE PROBLEM OF DISCRIMINATION

Chapter 2

The Policy Bases for Antidiscrimination Law

B. ARE ANTIDISCRIMINATION LAWS NECESSARY TO ELIMINATE DISCRIMINATION?

Page 55.   Add at end of carryover paragraph:

See also David Charny & G. Mitu Gulati, Efficiency-Wages, Tournaments, and Discrimination: A Theory of Employment Discrimination Law for High-Level Jobs, 33 Harv. C.R.–C.L. L. Rev. 57, 68 (1998) (arguing that in high-level jobs, "difficulties in monitoring (or, equivalently, discretion by managers in evaluating workers) create powerful opportunities for discriminatory hiring and promotion").

D. THE COSTS AND BENEFITS OF PROHIBITING DISCRIMINATION

1. Weighing Economic Costs and Benefits

Page 79. Add new Note 2A after carryover paragraph:

2A. Recent scholarship has considered whether the differences between age discrimination and race/gender discrimination require reconsidering of the rules governing age discrimination. Professor George Rutherglen, From Race to Age: The Expanding Scope of Employment Discrimination Laws, 24 J. Leg. Stud. 491 (1995), questioned the underlying basis of the ADEA. Taking up this theme, Samuel Issacharoff and Erica Worth Harris, Is Age Discrimination Really Age Discrimination?: The ADEA's Unnatural Solution, 72 N.Y.U. L. Rev. 780 (1997), argued that the elderly do not fit into the usual antidiscrimination model because "far from being discrete and insular, the elderly represent the normal unfolding of life's processes for all persons. As a group, older Americans do not suffer from poverty or face the disabling social stigma characteristically borne by black Americans. . . ." Id. at 781. Their article does not recommend repeal of the statute but rather proposes modifying the law (as by restricting disparate impact analysis) to recognize that "the dramatic shift in wealth towards older Americans and the diminished job prospects of the young provoke grave concern that a misguided antidiscrimination model has allowed a concerted and politically powerful group of Americans to engage in a textbook example of what economists would term 'rent-seeking.'" Id. at 783.

Professor Christine Jolls, Hands-Tying and the Age Discrimination in Employment Act, 74 Tex. L. Rev. 1813 (1996), agrees that the traditional justifications for antidiscrimination legislation may not apply to the ADEA. However, she argues that the statute may prevent employer opportunism. The empirical observation that older workers are often paid more for doing the same work as younger employees may simply reflect a preference by both workers and employers for wages to rise over time. Such a preference, however, can only be achieved if employers can tie their own hands, i.e., avoid the temptations of opportunistically replacing expensive, older workers with cheaper, younger ones. The ADEA, by providing legal protection for older workers, provides this "hands-tying." This analysis may justify the application of disparate impact to age cases.

PART II

THE CONCEPT OF DISCRIMINATION UNDER TITLE VII, THE AGE DISCRIMINATION IN EMPLOYMENT ACT, AND SECTION 1981

Chapter 3

Individual Disparate
Treatment Discrimination

B. THE MEANING OF
DISCRIMINATION INTENT

Page 100.   Add at end of Note 3:

See also Floyd D. Weatherspoon, Remedying Employment Discrimination
Against African-American Males: Stereotypical Biases Engender a Case of
Race Plus Sex Discrimination, 36 Wash. L. J. 23 (1996) (arguing that African-
American males are victims of race and sex discrimination that should be recognized as separate from either race or sex discrimination claims); Tanya Ka-
teri Hernandez, "Multiracial" Discourse: Racial Classification in an Era of
Color-Blind Jurisprudence, 57 Md. L. Rev. 97 (1998) (arguing that mixed-
race census count will not overcome racism but rather will reinforce the current judicial negation of the experiences of racial discrimination against persons of color and therefore maintain a system of race-based privilege); e.
christi cunningham, The Rise of Identity Politics I: The Myth of the Pro-

tected Class in Title VII Disparate Treatment Cases, 30 Conn. L. Rev. 441 (1998) (arguing that using protected class analysis restricts scope of Title VII by compartmentalizing the identity of individuals).

Page 112. Add new note 8A at end of page:

8A. Suppose an employer asks an older worker about her plans for retirement. Does this suggest age discrimination? See Cox v. Dubuque Bank & Trust Co., 113 F.3d 492 (8th Cir. 1998) (in ADEA action, employer was entitled jury instruction that it had a right to make reasonable inquiries into employee's retirement plans).

Page 115. Add new Note 16A after first full paragraph:

16A. Gary Minda, Opportunistic Downsizing of Aging Workers: The 1990's Version of Age and Pension Discrimination in Employment, 48 Hastings L.J. 511 (1997). Professor Minda argues that opportunistic downsizing is a unique form of disparate treatment based on age that conflicts with the congressional purpose underlying both ADEA and ERISA because older workers are particularly vulnerable. Id. at 513. Such actions violate the ADEA when the employer's decision to downsize older, late-career workers is motivated by the higher salaries and benefits such workers earn due to seniority. Id. at 513-514. Taking issue with Michael J. Zimmer, The Emerging Uniform Structure of Disparate Treatment Discrimination Litigation, 30 Ga. L. Rev. 563, 573 (1996), Professor Minda writes:

> . . . According to [one] view, *Biggins* rules out the possibility of using salary and pension as a "proxy" for proving age discrimination. A prime advocate of this view is Michael Zimmer, who has recently argued that *Biggins* creates two serious impediments to age discrimination claims. First, it makes it easier for employers to defend against a claim at the rebuttal stage. Instead of producing evidence that they had "legitimate, nondiscriminatory reasons" for their actions, employers can now satisfy their burden by producing evidence of any reason so long as the reason is not age. . . . The second impediment established by *Biggins*, according to Zimmer, is that the decision has restricted the "range of circumstantial evidence upon which a fact finder can draw the inference of discrimination." In refusing to allow the *Biggins* plaintiff to prove age discrimination on the basis of the employer's pension interference, the Court seemingly ruled out the possibility of proving unlawful motive through circumstantial evidence based on an accumulation of years of service. . . . If Zimmer's interpretation of *Biggins* is followed, then ADEA would be of little help to older workers who lose their jobs whenever their employer has any other non-age reasons of terminating employment. Pension status or length of service could not be used as proxies for age, even though there might be a positive correlation between pension status or length of service and age. In restricting the

C. Inferential Evidence of Discriminatory Intent

range of circumstantial evidence, *Biggins* has potentially opened the door for employers to escape ADEA liability by using length of service, pension status, and salary level as non-discriminatory proxies for firing older workers.

Id. at 536-537. Professor Minda proffers an alternative reading of *Biggins*, one that is more optimistic about the possibility of establishing age discrimination claims on the basis of salary and pension status. He looks to the language in the case — "Pension status may be a proxy for age, not in the sense that ADEA makes the two factors equivalent, but in the sense that the employer may suppose a *correlation* between the two factors and act accordingly." Professor Minda then argues that the ADEA protects older workers who are fired because their salary is higher than their productivity. See also Stewart Schwab, Life-Cycle Justice: Accommodating Just Cause and Employment at Will, 92 Mich. L. Rev. 8 (1993). Professor Minda does note that the Seventh Circuit has interpreted *Biggins* to support Zimmer's conclusion. EEOC v. Francis W. Parker Sch., 41 F.3d 1073, 1076 (7th Cir. 1994), *cert. denied*, 515 U.S. 1142 (1995). Are you persuaded that Zimmer has overstated the effect of *Biggins?*

C. INFERENTIAL EVIDENCE OF DISCRIMINATORY INTENT

1. The Plaintiff's Prima Facie Case

Page 124.   Add new Note 3A:

3A. In Coco v. Elmwood Care, Inc., 128 F.3d 1177 (7th Cir. 1997), a discharge case, the court required that plaintiff, who showed he was replaced by a younger worker, also show that he was meeting the employer's expectations for the job:

> If your job is to document maintenance problems, arrange for their correction, and conduct fire drills, and you fail to do these things, you are not performing up to your employer's legitimate expectations, and that is the end of your case if *McDonnell Douglas* is all that you have to go on. *McDonnell Douglas* is for cases in which an employee is performing in a satisfactory manner but loses his job anyway and is replaced by someone belonging to a different group from his own; in such a case there is sufficient likelihood of discrimination to make it reasonable to require the defendant to produce evidence of a noninvidious reason for the "discrimination."

Id. at 1180. Does this mean that employees with less than spotless records in effect lose their protection against discrimination?

Page 126.   Add at end of first paragraph of Note 7:

Beaird v. Seagate Tech., 145 F.3d 1159, 1167 (10th Cir. 1998), found that plaintiffs made out a prima facie case of age discrimination in an RIF by showing that, as to each of the plaintiffs, at least one younger employee was retained in the same job:

> [T]he fourth element . . . should be understood to parallel the fourth element of *McDonnell Douglas* by eliminating "lack of vacancy" as a legitimate nondiscriminatory motive for the employment decision. . . . [It] should not be understood to require a plaintiff to produce evidence that age was a determining factor in the employer's motivation. Such an understanding would effectively fuse the prima facie and pretext steps of *McDonnell Douglas* and "obviate[] the central purpose behind the *McDonnell Douglas* method, which is to relieve the plaintiff of the burden of having to uncover what is very difficult to uncover — evidence of discriminatory intent."

Page 126.   Add new Note 7A:

7A.   e. christi cunningham, The Rise of Identity Politics I: The Myth of the Protected Class in Title VII Disparate Treatment Cases, 30 Conn. L. Rev. 441, 442-443 (1998), analyzes the first element of *McDonnell Douglas* — membership in a protected class — arguing that "as applied, the criterion serves as a standing requirement that unnecessarily defines plaintiffs as specially protected members of a defined group by categories of discrimination rather than as individuals who are unfairly disadvantaged in the workplace" by discrimination made illegal by Title VII. She goes on to protest this fracturing of the identity of plaintiffs.

Page 127.   Add at end of carryover paragraph:

Enowmbitang v. Seagate Tech., 148 F.3d 970, 973 (8th Cir 1998) (employer's failure to provide plaintiff with a computer "does not rise above a 'mere inconvenience' and therefore does not constitute adverse employment action . . . whether Seagate wishes to give its technicians specific pieces of equipment is a business decision that is not susceptible to judicial oversight"); Ledergerber v. Strangler, 122 F.3d 1142 (8th Cir. 1997) (replacement of personal staff and placing employer's standard antidiscriminatory statement in personnel file did not constitute adverse employment since employee's position was not affected). But see Theresa M. Beiner, Do Reindeer Games Count as Terms, Conditions or Privileges of Employment Under Title VII?, 37 B.C. L. Rev. 643 (1996) (arguing that "reindeer games," benefits such as golf games and lunches accorded to male employees but not to females, are terms and conditions of employment; denying access to such benefits to women should be treated similarly to a hostile work environment). See gen-

C. Inferential Evidence of Discriminatory Intent

erally Rebecca Hanner White, De Minimis Discrimination, 47 Emory L. J. 1121 (1998).

Page 133.   Add at end of Note 2:

Anderson v. Conboy, 156 F.3d 167 (2d Cir. 1998), held that § 1981 prohibits discrimination on the basis of alienage as well as race and that, after its amendment by the 1991 Civil Rights Act, proscribes such discrimination by private as well as public actors.

Page 137.   Add at end of Note 11:

But see Ann C. McGinley, The Emerging Cronyism Defense and Affirmative Action: A Critical Perspective on the Distinction Between Colorblind and Race Conscious Decision Making Under Title VII, 39 Ariz. L. Rev. 1003 (1997) (arguing that recent Supreme Court cases have unreasonably narrowed the intent requirement in Title VII law, permitting the emergence of the cronyism defense; the cronyism defense exalts the employer's liberty interest over an employee's right to equality in hiring); see also Ann C. McGinley, Rethinking Civil Rights and Employment at Will, 57 Ohio St. L.J. 1443 (1996).

Page 137.   Add new Note 11A:

11A. In Deffenbaugh-Williams v. Wal-Mart Stores, Inc., 156 F.3d 581 (5th Cir. 1998), the employer argued that a white plaintiff, claiming discrimination because of her interracial relationship, failed to show that she was a member of a class protected by Title VII. Finding that Title VII prohibits discrimination premised on an interracial relationship, the court rejected Wal-Mart's argument. "[W]e disagree with Wal-Mart's quite strained assertion that the relevant protected class is blacks. Deffenbaugh, who is white, alleged that she was fired because she was engaged in an interracial relationship. . . . [A]ssuming sufficient supporting evidence, a reasonable juror could find that Deffenbaugh was discriminated against because of her race (white), if that discrimination was premised on the fact that she, a white person, had a relationship with a black person."

Page 139.   Add at end of Note 14:

Taken v. Oklahoma Corp. Comm'n, 125 F.3d 1366, 1369 (9th Cir. 1997), held that members of groups that have historically been *favored* in employment are not entitled to the *McDonnell Douglas* presumption unless they prove "background circumstances that support an inference that the defendant is one of those unusual employers who discriminates against the majority."

11

Page 144. Add at end of Note 2:

See also Jones v. Bessemer Carraway Med. Ctr., 137 F.3d 1306 (11th Cir. 1998) (judgment as a matter of law affirmed when trial judge at close of trial decided that plaintiff had failed to establish a prima facie case).

Page 145. Add at end of Note 3:

Fisher v. Vassar College, 114 F.3d 1332 (2d Cir. 1997)(en banc), *cert. denied*, 118 S. Ct. 851 (1998), (finding of liability under Title VII supported by a prima facie case and a sustainable finding of pretext was subject to the clearly erroneous standard of review).

Page 146. Add at end of Note 7:

In Smith v. Borough of Wilkinsburg, 147 F.3d 272 (3d Cir. 1998), a jury verdict for defendant was reversed because of error in instructions:

> "[T]he jury must be given the legal context in which it is to find and apply the facts . . . [T]he jurors must be instructed that they are entitled to infer, but need not, that the plaintiff's ultimate burden of demonstrating intentional discrimination by a preponderance of the evidence can be met if they find that the facts needed to make up the prima facie case have been established and they disbelieve the employer's explanation for its decision.

Id. at 279. In the accompanying footnote 4, the court added that "this does not mean that the instruction should include the technical aspects of the *McDonnell Douglas* burden shifting, a charge reviewed as unduly confusing and irrelevant for a jury." Id. In contrast, the Seventh Circuit reached the opposite conclusion, finding that jury instructions that failed to allocate the burdens are not fatal to a jury verdict as long as the jury understood that its task was to decide who told the truth about what happened. Anchor v. Riverside Golf Club, 117 F.3d 339 (7th Cir. 1997).

Page 147. Add new Note 8A after carryover paragraph:

8A. Egbuna v. Time-Life Libraries, Inc, 153 F.3d 184 (4th Cir. 1998), held that a former employee who was an alien without work authorization was not "qualified" for any position at the time reemployment was sought and, thus, had no cause of action. Is this holding consistent with McKennon v. Nashville Publishing Co., reproduced at page 1232, which holds that an after-discovered legitimate reason for discharge merely limits the remedies of the plaintiff and does not foreclose the claim?

C. Inferential Evidence of Discriminatory Intent

2. *Defendant's Rebuttal and Plaintiff's Proof of Pretext*

Page 152.   Add new Note 6A:

6A. What is the impact of the employer's breach of its own policies or practices? In Carter v. Three Springs Res. Treatment, 132 F.3d 635 (11th Cir. 1998), the court reversed summary judgment for the employer in a failure to promote case. "Carter proved that Three Springs had a policy of posting job vacancies, not adhered to in this case. We have held that the failure to promulgate hiring and promotion policies can be circumstantial evidence of discrimination. . . . Certainly, it is even more suspicious where it is alleged that established rules were bent or broken to give a non-minority applicant an edge in the hiring process." Id. at 644. Lyoch v. Anheuser-Busch Cos., 139 F.3d 612 (8th Cir. 1998), also reversed summary judgment for the employer where plaintiff showed the criteria for promotion were subjective. "The depositions of . . . two long-time Anheuser-Busch employees who served in several managerial positions, support Lyoch's argument that Anheuser-Busch's promotion policy was informal and subjective and . . . 'vague and secretive.' According to [one], he did not formally apply for new positions at Anheuser-Busch; he was simply asked if he would be interested or informed that he would be promoted." Id at 615.

Page 152.   Insert in second to last line before "Assuming":

This theory that an employer who hires an older employee is unlikely to then develop an aversion to his age has now been embraced by the majority of circuits. E.g., Brown v. CSC Logic, Inc., 82 F.3d 651 (5th Cir. 1996); Hartsel v. Keys, 87 F.3d 795 (6th Cir. 1996); Rand v. CF Indus., Inc., 42 F.3d 1139 (7th Cir. 1994). Sometimes labeled the "same actor interference" or the "*Proud* presumption," a strong inference is created that discrimination was not a determinative factor for an adverse action taken by an employer who had hired that person a relatively short time previously. But see Waldron v. SL Industries, Inc., 56 F.3d 491 (3d Cir. 1995) (that hirer and firer are the same and discharge occurred shortly after hiring is simply evidence like any other and should not be accorded any presumptive value). See also Madel v. FCI Mktg., Inc., 116 F.3d 1247 (8th Cir. 1997) (presumption inappropriate where evidence of overt discrimination exists).

Several circuits have applied this inference to discrimination cases outside the ADEA. See, e.g., Jaques v. Clean-Up Group, Inc., 57 F.3d 506 (1st Cir. 1996) (disability discrimination); Jiminez v. Mary Washington College, 57 F.3d 369 (4th Cir. 1995) (race and national origin discrimination); Bradley v. Harcourt, Brace and Co., 104 F.3d 267 (9th Cir. 1996) (sex discrimination). Although this inference is normally applied when there has been a short span of time between the hiring and the adverse action, at least one circuit has held that a relatively brief period is not an absolute requirement. See Buhrmaster v. Overnite Transp. Co., 61 F.3d 461 (6th Cir. 1995) (upholding a jury instruction on the same actor inference: "time weakens the same actor inference, it does not destroy it . . . a short period of time is not an essential element where plaintiff's class does not change."). See generally, Julie S. Northrop, The Same Actor Inference in Employment Discrimination: Cheap Justice, 73 Wash. L. Rev. 193 (1998).

Page 154. Add at end of Note 13:

In Beaird v. Seagate Technology, 145 F.3d 1159, 1168 (10th Cir. 1998), a RIF case, the court wrote that a plaintiff can demonstrate pretext in three ways:

> First, she can argue that her own termination does not accord with the RIF criteria supposedly employed. . . .
> Second, a plaintiff can adduce evidence that her evaluation under the defendant's RIF criteria was deliberately falsified or manipulated so as to effect her termination or otherwise adversely alter her employment status. . . . One method of demonstrating manipulation or falsification of evaluation is to produce evidence that a supervisor responsible for assessing her performance displayed ageist animus.
> Third, a plaintiff can adduce evidence that the RIF is more generally pretextual. For instance, a plaintiff may establish that an employer actively sought to replace a number of RIF-terminated employees with new hires. . . . Statistical evidence may, in certain circumstances, be relevant to this purpose. . . . Contrary to defendant's argument, however, statistical evidence cannot defeat the pretext claim of an individual plaintiff where the plaintiff's case rests on non-statistical evidence.

Page 157. Add new Note 16A:

16A. While plaintiff's attorneys are trying to ferret out evidence of discriminatory motives, the prospects of exposure for discrimination and other employment litigation have led to increasing efforts to "bulletproof" employment decisions. Management attorneys have increasingly trained and counseled employers about discharging or disciplining workers in a manner which limits liability. Are such programs effective ways to achieve compliance with the statute, or ways to immunize discriminatory decisions, or perhaps both? See generally Susan Bisom-Rapp, Bullet-Proofing the Workplace: Symbol and Substance in Employment Discrimination Law Practice, 26 Fla. St. U. L. Rev. ___, ___ (1999) (while litigation prevention strategies developed by defense firms for employers "may prompt managers to identify and remedy certain biased actions, it is equally possible that preventive practices mask rather than eliminate some discriminatory decisions.").

C. Inferential Evidence of Discriminatory Intent

Page 168.   Add at end of Note 2:

The debate continues. Mark S. Brodin, The Demise of Circumstantial Proof in Employment Discrimination Litigation: *St. Mary's Honor Center v. Hicks*, Pretext, and the "Personality" Excuse, 18 Berkeley J. Emp. & Lab. L 183 (1997), attacks *Hicks* for violating "two of the most basic tenets of American procedure . . . first, that the court is a passive tribunal, not an active player in the construction of arguments and theories, and second, that cases are to be decided solely on the basis of the evidence presented, not the conjecture of the fact-finder." Id. at 209-210. More broadly, he concludes that *Hicks* "stands as a veritable guide for avoiding liability. Title VII should not become the vehicle for legitimating the very conduct it is directed towards prohibiting." Id. at 239. See also William R. Corbett, Of Babies, Bathwater, and Throwing Out Proof Structures: It Is Not Time to Jettison *McDonnell Douglas*, 2 Employee Rts. & Employment Policy J. 361 (1998), (criticizing *Hicks* as well as Professor Malamud's proposal to abandon *McDonnell Douglas*); Ruth Gana Okediji, Status Rules: Doctrine as Discrimination in a Post-*Hicks* Environment, 26 Fla. St. L. Rev. 49 (1998); Stephen Plass, Truth: The Last Virtue in Title VII Litigation, 29 Seton Hall L. Rev. 599 (1998) (pointing out that, contrary to Justice Scalia's claim that even perjury does not warrant a verdict, *employee* lies in litigation are often outcome-determinative, including dismissal of their cases).

Page 170.   Add new Notes 8A through 8E:

8A. McCullough v. Real Foods, 140 F.3d 1123 (8th Cir. 1998), reversed summary judgment for the employer. The court nevertheless found that, once defendant's rebuttal was carried, "[t]he burden then shifts back to the plaintiff to present evidence sufficient to support two findings. . . . First, the plaintiff must present evidence which creates a fact issue as to whether the employer's proffered reasons are mere pretext. . . . Second, she must present evidence which creates a reasonable inference that the adverse employment decision was an act of intentional racial discrimination." Id. at 1127. Must plaintiff prove pretext to win a *McDonnell Douglas* case? After *Hicks*, it is necessary, but also sufficient, for plaintiff to convince the factfinder that there was discrimination. Why must plaintiff also prove pretext?

8B. In Fisher v. Vassar College, 114 F.3d 1332 (2d Cir. 1997) (en banc), *cert. denied*, 118 S. Ct. 851 (1998), the court decided that liability under Title VII supported by a prima facie case and a sustainable finding of pretext was subject to the clearly erroneous standard of review. The court, however, was severely split, rendering five opinions covering some sixty pages. The case involved a college professor who claimed she was denied tenure because of her status as a married woman. Judges Jacobs and Leval, writing for six members of the court, described how *McDonnell Douglas* differs from the general notions of the effect of a prima facie case:

> "Prima facie case" denotes what evidence a plaintiff must offer to avoid dismissal after presentation of the plaintiff's direct case. Except as to causes of actions for which special rules have been adopted, to satisfy the requirements of the prima facie case the plaintiff must present evidence from which a factfinder could reasonably find every element that the plaintiff must ultimately prove to prevail in the action. . . . Because of the Supreme Court's adoption of a particular framework in *McDonnell Douglas* and *Burdine,* the same is not true of a discrimination case: a plaintiff alleging discrimination can satisfy the prima facie case and avoid dismissal at the conclusion of the plaintiff's direct case without submitting evidence sufficient to support a finding in his favor on each element that the plaintiff must ultimately prove to win. The burden-shifting presumption excuses the plaintiff at that stage from showing that discrimination was present and caused the adverse employment action plaintiff suffered. If the plaintiff submits evidence of the minimal elements of the special discrimination prima facie case — membership in the protected class, qualification, adverse employment action, and preference for someone outside the protected class — the remaining elements (discrimination and causation) are presumed at this stage of the litigation, and defendant must take up the burden of going forward.
>
> But as *Burdine* and *St. Mary's* make clear, the presumption disappears once the employer has proffered a reason. When the presumption drops away, plaintiff's burden is enlarged to include every element of the claim. Discrimination and cause are no longer presumed. To sustain the burden of putting forth a case that can support a verdict in his favor, plaintiff must then (unlike the prima facie stage) point to sufficient evidence to reasonably support a finding that he was harmed by the employer's illegal discrimination. . . . It can be readily seen, furthermore, that the essential elements of this diminished, minimal prima facie case do not necessarily support a reasonable inference of illegal discrimination. In our diverse workplace, virtually any decision in which one employment applicant is chosen from a pool of qualified candidates will support a slew of prima facie cases of discrimination. The rejected candidates are likely to be older, or to differ in race, religion, sex, and national origin from the chosen candidate. Each of these differences will support a prima facie case of discrimination, even though a review of the full circumstances may conclusively show that illegal discrimination played no part whatever in the selection.

Id. at 1337. Judge Winter, writing in dissent for four members of the court, disagreed.

> "Prima facie case" has two meanings, one stronger than the other: (i) the plaintiff has produced evidence sufficient to establish a disputed fact from which, if credited by the trier, arises a rebuttable presumption — the strong version; or (ii) the plaintiff has produced evidence sufficient to permit, but not compel, a trier of fact to find a disputed fact for the plaintiff — the weak ver-

C. Inferential Evidence of Discriminatory Intent

sion. . . . Under *McDonnell Douglas*, a prima facie case is initially of the stronger (i) variety. If the employer remains silent and the trier finds the facts that trigger the *McDonnell Douglas* presumption, the employer loses. . . . Once the employer proffers a lawful reason for the employment decision then the "presumption [of unlawful discrimination] drops out." The majority opinion holds that when the "presumption . . . drops out," proof of the *McDonnell Douglas* four factors without more no longer constitutes a prima facie case of discrimination. . . .

In my view, the "drops out" language indicates only that the *McDonnell Douglas* rebuttable presumption, version (i), loses all evidentiary weight, leaving a prima facie case in the sense of version (ii). . . . "Prima facie case" and "presumption" are not synonymous. The term prima facie case, even when used in sense (ii), means that a party having the burden of persuasion regarding a disputed fact has presented legally sufficient evidence to allow the trier of fact to find that fact.

Presumptions, on the other hand, are legal rules calling upon the trier to add weight to one party's evidentiary scale if the evidence of the basis facts triggering the presumption is sufficient to allow the trier to find those facts. . . . To say that a "presumption . . . drops out," therefore, does not inexorably mean that there is no longer legally sufficient evidence — i.e., a prima facie case — to allow a trier to find the disputed fact; it may mean only that the trier now resolves the issue based on their view of the evidence as a whole without giving the facts constituting the prima face case the added evidentiary weight that they formerly had.

Id. at 1386.

8C. The *Fisher* majority also described the effect of a showing that the employer's reason was pretextual:

A showing that the defendant's proffered reason for the adverse employment action is not the real reason may serve as evidence that the defendant intentionally discriminated. We attach the label "pretext" to a proffered reason that is not credited by the finder of fact. But the label "pretext" does not answer the question: pretext for what? In some cases, an employer's proffered reason is a mask for unlawful discrimination. But discrimination does not lurk behind every inaccurate statement. Individual decision-makers may intentionally dissemble in order to hide a reason that is non-discriminatory but unbecoming or small-minded, such as back-scratching, log-rolling, horse-trading, institutional politics, envy, nepotism, spite, or personal hostility. In short, the fact that the proffered reason was false does not necessarily mean that the true motive was the illegal one argued by the plaintiff. . . .

Once the trial has moved to the stage at which the plaintiff must prove discrimination by a preponderance of the evidence, a defendant's false statements are nothing more than pieces of circumstantial evidence, which may be employed, as in many other types of cases, to reveal the speaker's state of mind. To the extent that an actor in defendant's position is unlikely to have proffered a false explanation except to conceal a discriminatory motive, then the false explanation will be powerful evidence of discrimination. On the other hand, if

17

the circumstances show that the defendant gave the false explanation to conceal something other than discrimination, the inference of discrimination will be weak or nonexistent. And if, on examination of the circumstances, there are many possible reasons for the false explanation, stated or unstated, and illegal discrimination is no more likely a reason than others, then the pretext gives minimal support to plaintiff's claim of discrimination . . .

Accordingly, a Title VII plaintiff may prevail only if an employer's proffered reasons are shown to be a pretext *for discrimination*, either because the pretext finding itself points to discrimination or because other evidence in the record points in that direction — or both.

Id. at 1337-38. What jury instruction should be given based on the law as set forth by the majority? Judge Winter's dissent takes issue with the majority: "This puzzling ruling is also at odds with a vast body of law allowing inferences of consciousness of guilt to be drawn from dishonest behavior concerning facts material to litigation. For example, it is — or was until now — settled law that a false exculpatory statement by a [criminal] defendant may (not must) support an inference of consciousness of guilt." Id. at 1390.

8D. In Beaird v. Seagate Tech., Inc, 145 F.3d 1159 (10th Cir. 1998), a reduction in force case, the majority said that, when a defendant asserted a facially non-discriminatory reason for the employee's termination, "The plaintiff may then resist summary judgment if she can present evidence that that proffered reason was pretextual, 'i.e., unworthy of belief,' see *Randle v. City of Aurora*, 69 F.3d 441, 451 (10th Cir. 1995). . . ." Id. at 1165. Judge Tacha dissented and argued that *Randle* interfered with the proper role of the trial judge to send only cases with material issues of fact to the jury.

> The question I raise here, then, is whether a plaintiff who has presented evidence from which a court could conclude that an employer's proffered non-discriminatory reason is pretextual (i.e., unworthy of belief) has necessarily established pretext upon which a jury could infer discriminatory motive. I think the answer to the question is clearly no. . . . If a plaintiff's evidence of pretext is not legally sufficient to support any inference of illegal discrimination, there is no genuine issue of any material fact, and the case should not go to the jury. . . . The rule in this Circuit, however, is that an employment discrimination suit will always go to the jury so long as the evidence is sufficient to allow the jury to disbelieve the employer's proffered reason for the employment action. . . . This *per se* rule precludes a district court from engaging in a separate inquiry into whether that evidence is legally sufficient to support a finding of discrimination. . . . Merely because a plaintiff has proffered evidence of pretext does not and should not mean that her evidence is necessarily legally sufficient to support a finding of discrimination.

Id. at 1177.
8E. A study by Julie Tang & Theodore M. Macmillan, Eighth Circuit Employment Discrimination Law: *Hicks* and Its Impact on Summary Judgment,

D. Direct Evidence of Discriminatory Intent

41 St. Louis U. L. J. 519, 533-534 (1997), summarized the Eighth Circuit's rules for granting summary judgment at the pretext stage.

> [A] plaintiff cannot overcome a defendant's motion for summary judgment at the pretext stage unless he or she can establish a genuine issue of material fact as to whether the defendant's proffered explanation constitutes the true reason for the defendant's adverse employment decision or is a pretext for discrimination. There are two simple yet important corollaries which must not be overlooked by the wary plaintiff. First, the plaintiff must show that the controversy, with respect to the ultimate issue of discrimination, is *genuine*. . . . Second, even if a genuine issue of fact can be established with respect to the truthfulness or credibility of the defendant's proffered explanation, the plaintiff must demonstrate that the controversy is *material* — in other words, that it tends to prove that the defendant was motivated by the protected factor (i.e., age, gender, etc.), not merely something which correlates with that factor. If a plaintiff fails to overcome either of these two hurdles, he or she will not be entitled to a trial on the merits. If, however, "the evidence considered in its entirety (1) creates a fact issue as to whether the employer's proffered reasons are pretextual *and* (2) creates a reasonable inference that [the protected factor] was a determinative factor in the adverse employment decision" — bearing in mind that the evidence relied upon by the plaintiff might, in some instances, serve "double duty" and establish both of these requirements and that the plaintiff need not necessarily directly disprove the defendant's proffered explanation — then the plaintiff is entitled to a jury trial on the merits. . . .

Consistent with sending such cases to the jury, the Eighth Circuit sitting en banc upheld a jury verdict for plaintiff, even though the defendant's proffered explanation — that it fired a sportscaster because of an unfavorable market survey about him — was based in fact and involved a legitimate business reason. Ryther v. KARE 11, 108 F.3d 832, 841 (8th Cir. 1997) (en banc) ("The jury had a right to believe that the survey was inadequate, biased [in the sense of unfavorable to the plaintiff] and in fact a subterfuge to mask KARE 11's age-biased animus" against plaintiff).

D. DIRECT EVIDENCE OF DISCRIMINATORY INTENT

Page 189. Add new Notes 2A and 2B:

2A. There is also the problem of what counts as a racial (or other) epithet. Debate broke out recently after Washington D.C.'s ombudsman, David Howard, used the word "Niggardly" to describe his reaction to a budget discussion. Niggardly, which means miserly or stingy, is derived from the Scandinavian and has no racial overtones or link to the racial slur it connotes. Apparently, use of the word offended a black colleague, causing him to storm out of the room before an explanation of the word's meaning could be given. Mr. Howard immediately resigned from his position, embarrassed for his insensitivity and poor judgment in using a word that could be so easily misconstrued. Some criticized the Mayor's hasty acceptance of Mr. Howard's resignation, viewing it as censorship of language based on other people's lack of understanding. But others applauded the Mayor's decision, recognizing a need for heightened sensitivity in regard to race relations. Melinda Henneberger, Race Mix-Up Raises Havoc for Capital, N.Y. Times, January 29, 1999, at A10. However, the Mayor, who asked Mr. Howard to return to his job, seems to agree with those who criticized his hasty acceptance of the aide's resignation. Mr. Howard accepted the offer to return, but requested a different assignment. Michael Janofsky, In a Word, Return, N.Y. Times, February 7, 1999 <http://nytimes.com>. Mr. Howard reported that he learned the word "niggardly" studying for his S.A.T. test during high school.

Some words cause offense, regardless of the speaker's intent or the technical meaning of the word. Presumably, the mere use of such a word could not be evidence of discriminatory intent under *Price Waterhouse*, no matter how offended listeners might be. But, of course, an individual's use of a word which he or she in fact realizes may cause offense could present a different problem. Some have argued that, because "niggardly" sounds too much like the racial slur "nigger," it should not be used, regardless of its literal correctness. Do you agree? In practice, this reasoning would require a heightened sensitivity to word usage and possible unintended racial connotations. It might also mean inferring discriminatory intent from knowing use of words others find offensive. Others argue "heightened sensitivity" is just another term for censorship. If some people's "hyper-sensitivity" forces others to change their speech, conversation will be impeded, and communication will be impaired. If this occurs only with a handful of phrases, the problems are minor; but many other phrases and terms were raised during the Howard debate as possibly causing offense to African Americans or other ethnic groups, including "spade" (as in, "to call a spade a spade"), "tarbaby," "denigrate," "spic and span," and "blackmail". The same argument applies to words with gender or sexual orientation connotations. "Fairy," "queen," "fag," and "queer" all connote both sexual orientation and far different meanings. As for gender itself, there are a myriad of words which could cause offense, depending on the meaning intended by the speaker or heard by the listener.

2B. There is also the question of the connection between the animus shown and the decision being challenged. In Jones v. Bessemer Carraway Med. Ctr., 137 F.3d 1306, 1322 n.1 (11th Cir. 1998), the trial court refused to admit the statements of plaintiff's supervisor because they were not immediately connected with the events leading to her discharge for insubordination. Those statements included "You black girls make me sick, sometimes I feel like just hitting you in the head," and "You black girls get away with every-

D. Direct Evidence of Discriminatory Intent

thing." The court affirmed judgment for defendant as a matter of law because, even if that evidence had been admitted, plaintiff would not have made out a prima facie case because there was no proof that similarly situated white employees were treated more favorably than plaintiff:

> It is this showing — and not the demonstration of racial animus alone — that addresses the fundamental issue in a Title VII disparate treatment case: "whether the defendant intentionally *discriminated* against the plaintiff . . ."
> Racial animus of a supervisor does not alleviate the need to satisfy the elements of a prima facie case, although statements showing some racial animus may be significant evidence of pretext once a plaintiff has set out the prima facie case.

Id. at 1313. Is this consistent with *Price Waterhouse?* But see Cordova v. State Farm Ins. Cos., 124 F.2d 1145, 1148-49 (9th Cir. 1997) (plaintiff can also establish a prima facie case "without satisfying the *McDonnell Douglas* test, if she provides evidence suggesting that the "employment decision was based on a discriminatory criterion").

Page 190.   Add at end of Note 3:

The Eighth Circuit recently adopted the *Ostrowski* approach in Deneen v. Northwest Airlines, 132 F.3d 431 (8th Cir. 1998), affirming a jury verdict that defendant had engaged in pregnancy discrimination:

> Direct evidence is that which demonstrates "a specific link between the alleged discriminatory animus and the challenged [employment] decision, sufficient to support a finding by a reasonable fact finder that an illegitimate criterion actually motivated [the employer's] decision" to take the adverse employment decision. . . . We conclude that the district court was correct in its determination that Mrs. Deneen presented direct evidence of discrimination: Without any real of knowledge of a physical limitation, Mr. Holmes stated that Ms. Deneen could not return to work from layoff status without a note from her physician because of her pregnancy-related condition. . . . Mr. Holmes's initial statement that she could not return to work was expressly based on her pregnancy-related condition, a condition he only assumed to exist, and was made before Mr. Holmes knew of any pregnancy-related physical restrictions. He did not simply refer to her pregnant status but made an adverse employment decision on the basis of his discriminatory judgment about her abilities or her propensity to use earned sick leave benefits.

Id at 436. Thus, the statement by the supervisor that plaintiff could not return to work without a doctor's note was direct evidence of pregnancy discrimination, even though it made no reference to pregnancy. Given the context, that statement was good circumstantial evidence.

In Thomas v. National Football League Players Assn., 131 F.3d 198 (D.C. Cir. 1997), the court described Justice O'Connor's use of the term "direct" evidence as including circumstantial evidence.

In our view, Justice O'Connor's invocation of "direct" evidence is not intended to disqualify circumstantial evidence nor to require that the evidence signify without inference. In context, the notion of "direct" evidence in Justice O'Connor's concurrence means only that the evidence marshaled in support of the substantiality of the discriminatory motive must actually relate to the question of discrimination in the particular employment decision, not to the mere existence of other, potentially unrelated, forms of discrimination in the workplace. Id. at 204.

In Indurante v. Local 705, International Brotherhood of Teamsters, 160 F.3d 364 (7th Cir. 1998), plaintiff was fired from his job in late 1994. While he claimed national origin discrimination, the defendant argued that Indurante was discharged because he was part of the "Ligurotis reign" and had to be removed to rid the union of corruption. Plaintiff submitted affidavits from former business agents that a newly appointed business agent, McCormick, had earlier said that "all Italians were going to be fired. . . . that all the Italians were nothing but mobsters and gangsters." The affidavit of another former business agent said, "In June, 1993, Trustee Burke told me that the plans were 'to get rid of all the Italians.'" Both McCormick and Burke played a role in Indurante's subsequent dismissal. Another former union organizer filed an affidavit that Trustee Zero, who made the decision to fire Indurante, had told him shortly afterwards that "the days of the goombahs are over." In nevertheless affirming summary judgment for defendant, the court described two approaches to determining what was direct evidence.

> The phrase "related to the employment decision in question" may simply mean that the comments should refer, first of all, to an employment decision, and second, to the same type of employment decision as the plaintiff is challenging. So comments about discrimination in hiring may not suffice if the case involves a discharge. But language in other cases goes further, suggesting that the comments should refer to the individual plaintiff's employment decision. . . . To the extent that the remarks ought to refer to Indurante's termination, that would pose a problem for Indurante's case: the remarks of Burke, McCormick and Zero were not made to Indurante and do not mention Indurante or his termination at all. In addition, the statements of Burke and McCormick are not contemporaneous with Indurante's firing: they come about 16 months earlier. . . . While Zero's purported remark — "the days of the goombahs are over" — does come fewer than five months after Indurante's firing, it was not even made to employees of the Local and does not expressly refer to employment.

Judge Rovner dissented:

> When two decisionmakers reveal that there is a plan in the works to get rid of the Italian-Americans, the omission to mention the plaintiff or his discharge in particular would seem to be a minor point — there is no dispute, after all, that Indurante is Italian-American, was perceived as such, and that he was indeed

D. Direct Evidence of Discriminatory Intent

terminated. That McCormick and Burke uttered these remarks sixteen months before Zero fired Indurante is a more salient observation, but one addressed to the ultimate weight of this evidence rather than to whether it is stray or on point. The fact is, some plans take a good while to carry out.

In contrast, in Harris v. Shelby County Bd. of Educ., 99 F.3d 1078, 1080 (11th Cir. 1996), the court defined direct evidence as "evidence, which if believed, proves the existence of fact in issue without inference or presumption." It then ruled that a statement by the school district superintendent — "we did not need to employ a black [as principal] at Thompson High School" — was *not* direct evidence that the school district did not pick plaintiff as principal because he was an African American. The statement, the court said, was not direct evidence since it "could by inference have more than one possible meaning." More recently, in Carter v. Three Springs Res. Treatment, 132 F.3d 635, 642 (11th Cir. 1998), the court rejected as direct evidence an affidavit of former worker that related a conversation with Ms. Cook, the manager who decided not to promote plaintiff, "identified [in herself] a bias against blacks and she found that they were difficult for her to trust or get along with":

> [T]he statement does not amount to direct evidence. First, the statement is susceptible to more than one interpretation. Cook, in explaining her bias to a black colleague, could have been expressing a desire to get past prior prejudices. We have held that statements that are open to more than one interpretation do not constitute direct evidence of racial discrimination . . . Second, the statement does not relate directly to the decision to promote Carter to the position of Program Directory. To say that Cook "identified a bias" to Allen is not the same as saying that Cook exercised that bias in the case of Carter's promotion. Direct evidence, by definition, is evidence that does not require such an inferential leap between fact and conclusion.

Page 195.   Add new Note 14A:

14A. In Galdieri-Ambrosini v. National Realty & Dev. Corp., 136 F.3d 276, 290 (2d Cir. 1998), the plaintiff, a secretary, claimed that she had been fired because she had been forced to do personal work for her boss, work which was stereotypical women's work:

> [V]irtually every task of which she complains was quintessential secretarial work: typing, copying, faxing, scheduling appointments, locating addresses or telephone numbers, handling telephone calls, and arranging for pick-ups and delivery. Evidence that a female secretary has been required to perform such services as typing her employer's personal letters or making appointments for him with the cable installer, in the absence of evidence that could permit an inference that gender played a role in those work assignments, is insufficient to permit a finding of gender bias.
> Here there was no evidence whatever that Simon, in making those assignments gave any consideration to Ambrosini's gender.

Page 201.   Add after carryover paragraph:

One recent case allowed the employer to avoid liability, despite the demonstrated racism of lower supervisors. The decisionmaker asked the employee to prove that she had been "set up" by one of those supervisors, but the employee failed to do so. Willis v. Marion Cty. Auditor's Office, 118 F.3d 542 (7th Cir 1997), upheld setting aside of a verdict for plaintiff:

> There is no dispute between the parties that, on at least three separate occasions, a first-line supervisor discovered tardy invoices in Ms. Willis' files or work areas. No party disputes that three such offenses would warrant dismissal under Marion County' personnel policy. The evidence presented to the jury permitted, although it did not compel the conclusions that Conklin and Hupp [two first-line supervisors] bore a great deal of ill will toward Ms. Willis because of her race and that Conklin had planted the invoices. This evidence, standing alone, is not a sufficient basis for the verdict. Statements by subordinates normally are not probative of an intent to retaliate by decisionmaker . . . Conklin and Hupp did not make the decision. Moreover, it is clear that Mizen accepted full responsibility for the decision and did not accept uncritically the assertions of her subordinates. When Ms. Willis alleged to Mizen that the first reprimand was bogus and a pretext for Conklin's racism, Mizen asked Ms. Willis to provide supporting materials that Conklin had planted the stray invoices to get Ms. Willis fired. Ms. Willis failed to provide any further information.. . . . There was also no evidence presented at trial that Mizen harbored a race-based animus toward Ms. Willis. . . .
>
> [T]here can be situations in which the forbidden motive a subordinate employee can be imputed to the employer because, under the circumstances of the case, the employer simply acted as the "cats's paw" of the subordinate. . . . However, it is clear that, when the causal relationship between the subordinate's illicit motive and the employer's ultimate decision is broken, and the ultimate decision is clearly made on the independent and a legally permissible basis, the bias of the subordinate is not relevant.

Id at 546. Such a view does not mean that such evidence is not admissible, only that it is not necessarily sufficient. In Griffin v. Washington Convention Cntr., 142 F.3d 1308 (D.C. Cir. 1998), the court found error in the exclusion of evidence that plaintiff's immediate supervisor was opposed to women working as electricians. "We hold that evidence of a subordinate's bias is relevant where, as here, the ultimate decisionmaker is not insulated from the subordinate's influence [where the immediate supervisor participated at every stage of the process that led to her termination]." Id at 1310.

In another case, Fisher v. Vassar College, 114 F.3d 1332 (2d Cir. 1997), *cert. denied*, 118 S. Ct. 851 (1998), the court commented that a system of multiple decision makers can too easily produce evidence of reasons for a decision that differ from the reason the employer claims to be the basis for the challenged decision. "Because there are numerous participants in the decision-making process [of granting tenure in a college], each potentially having individual reasons for rejecting a plaintiff, there is a greater likelihood that some of those reasons will differ from the reason officially given by the institution." Id. at 1338. In accompanying footnote 4, the court further commented: "The involvement of multiple decision-makers increases the likelihood that the institution's stated reason may differ from the true reasons held by some of the decision-makers — without increasing the likelihood that discrimination played any role in their decision." Id.

Page 202.   Add to last full paragraph:

; Johnson v. City of Fort Lauderdale, 148 F.3d 1228 (11th Cir. 1997) (Civil Rights Act of 1991 did not implicitly render Title VII and § 1981 the exclusive remedies for employment discrimination by municipality and its employees, thereby displacing parallel constitutional remedies under § 1983). See also Beardsley v. Webb, 30 F.3d 524 (4th Cir. 1994).

E.   IS A NEW STRUCTURE OF INDIVIDUAL DISPARATE TREATMENT THEORY EMERGING?

Page 228.   Add at the end of Note 11:

In Harris v. Shelby County Bd. of Educ., 99 F.3d 1078, 1080 (11th Cir. 1996), the Eleventh Circuit defined direct evidence as "evidence, which if believed, proves the existence of fact in issue without inference or presumption." It then ruled that a statement by the school district superintendent — "we did not need to employ a black [as principal] at Thompson High School" — was *not* direct evidence that the school district did not pick plaintiff as principal because he was an African American. The statement, the court said, "could by inference have more than one possible meaning." Id. at 1083. Nevertheless, the court remanded for the trial court to determine, pursuant to § 703(m), whether, based on that and other circumstantial evidence, "discrimination based on his race was one motivating factor behind [the superintendent's] decision not to recommend him." Id. Thus, this court appeared to apply § 703(m) to both *Price Waterhouse* and *McDonnell Douglas* cases.

In contrast, in Deneen v. Northwest Airlines, 132 F.3d 431, 436 (8th Cir. 1998), a female employee claimed that Northwest Airlines discriminated against her on the basis of her pregnancy. The court defined direct evidence very broadly, as evidence that "demonstrates a specific link between the alleged discriminatory animus and the challenged decision, sufficient to support a finding by a reasonable fact finder that an illegitimate criterion actually motivated the employer's decision." Under that broad definition, the employer's requirement that the pregnant plaintiff obtain a doctor's note before she could return to work was direct evidence of discrimination. Such a broad test of direct evidence appears to include most circumstantial evidence, because §703(m) would apply to a larger number of situations under this analysis.

In brief, the Eighth Circuit appears to treat evidence as direct in order to have §703(m) apply, and the Eleventh Circuit appears to treat most evidence as circumstantial, yet it also finds that §703(m) applies.

The Second Circuit has its own approach. In Fields v. New York State Office of Mental Retardation and Developmental Disabilities, 115 F.3d 116 (2d Cir. 1997), plaintiff argued that the 1991 Civil Rights Act abolished the distinction between *Price Waterhouse* and *McDonnell Douglas*. The court rejected the argument. First, it found that, even before the 1991 Act, the level of showing required of plaintiff in a *McDonnell Douglas* case was "a motivating factor" or "a substantial motivating factor." Thus, the 1991 Act amendments confirm "the prior understanding that a Title VII plaintiff wins by proving that an impermissible reason was 'a motivating factor' for an adverse employment decision." Id. at 123. Second, the only real effect of the 1991 amendments is to modify "*Price Waterhouse* to make sure that a successful affirmative defense only limits the plaintiff's relief, rather than avoiding the defendant's liability." Id. at 124. Under *Fields*, plaintiff need only prove race or gender to be "a motivating factor" without regard to the type of evidence in the record, which is the showing provided for in §703(m). But the §703(g)(2)(B) affirmative defense is applicable only if plaintiff has introduced direct or circumstantial-plus evidence. Why would the defendant be given an affirmative defense that is only available when plaintiff has high quality, more probative evidence of discrimination than in the simple *McDonnell Douglas* case? See also Thomas v. National Football Players Assn., 131 F.3d 198, 203, n. 1. (D.C. Cir. 1998), a retaliation case, in which the court indicated that §703(g)(2)(b) provided that "in which there is a finding of discriminatory motive and also a finding that the firing would have occurred even absent discrimination, the trial judge has discretion to grant some limited forms of relief: injunctive or declaratory relief, and attorney's fees, but not damages."

Page 228.   Add new Note 11A:

11A. Harris v. Shelby County Bd. of Educ., 99 F.3d 1078, 1080 (11th Cir. 1996), remanded for a §703(m) determination whether the decision not to recommend plaintiff for a school principal's job violated the statute. The court, however, upheld judgment for the defendant on its §706(g)(2)(B) affirmative defense: Defendant proved that the person defendant hired to be principal was so superior to plaintiff in terms of qualifications that it would have made the same decision even if it had not discriminated against plaintiff because of his race.

Chapter 4

Systemic Disparate Treatment Discrimination

C. PATTERNS AND PRACTICES OF DISCRIMINATION

Page 278.   Add at end of Note 3:

See also Maitland v. University of Minnesota, 153 F.3d 1013 (8th Cir. 1998).

D. DEFENSES TO DISPARATE TREATMENT CASES

1.   *Rebutting the Inference of Discriminatory Intent*

Page 311.   Add new Note 13A:

13A. Mary Anne C. Case Disaggregating Gender from Sex and Sexual Orientation: The Effeminate Man in the Law and Feminist Jurisprudence,

105 Yale L.J. 1, 37-38 (1995), argues that choosing "masculine" characteristic for jobs can itself be challenged. She describes four generations of sex-stereotyping cases:

> Briefly stated, the first generation focused on the assumption that an entire sex conformed to gender stereotypes; the second on the assumption that individual members of the sex did; the third on individuals penalized because their gender behavior did not conform to stereotypical expectations. Fourth-generation stereotyping claims, of the sort I endorse in this Article, might take on the stereotyping of the job and its requirements rather than of the person holding or applying for it, challenging the assumption that qualities gendered masculine (or, more rarely, feminine) are essential to success rather than demanded merely by stereotypical expectations.

Professor Case argues that this use of gendered expectations can be challenged under disparate impact theory. But why isn't disparate treatment available?

2.   Bona Fide Occupational Qualifications

Page 346.   Add new Note 6A:

6A. The Hooters chain of restaurants hires only women, who are scantily clad, to serve food to customers. The company defended its practice by arguing that, "A lot of places serve good burgers. The Hooters' Girls, with their charm and All-American sex appeal, are what our customers come for." N.Y. Times, Nov. 16, 1995, at A20, col. 5. The EEOC dropped its investigation against Hooters after the company's massive public relations campaign. A private action was then settled, under terms which allowed Hooters to continue to hire only women as waitpersons. The men who were discriminated against by this company policy did, however, receive monetary compensation. Hooters to Pay $3.75 Million in Sex Suit, USA Today, Oct. 1, 1997, at 1A. Is selling sex appeal a BFOQ?

Page 347.   Add to note 9 before "Kim Dayton":

Suzanne Samuels, The Lasting Legacy of International Union, U.A.W. v. Johnson Controls: Equal Employment and Workplace Health and Safety Five Years Later, 12 Wis. Women's L.J. 1 (1997), "If anything, the decision moved the issue of workplace hazards off of the public agenda without ever really addressing it. In this way, Johnson Controls, while a victory for workers and women who sought entry into jobs that had been closed to them, was in fact a staggering defeat. Johnson Controls took the pressure off of employers and policy-makers to deal with the problem of workplace reproductive and devel-

D. Defenses to Disparate Treatment Cases

opmental hazards by simply declaring that employees could decide whether to expose themselves to the risk of reproductive and fetal harm."

Page 349. Add at end of Note 13:

In Robino v. Iranon, 145 F.3d 1109, 1109 (9th Cir. 1998), at issue was a rule, like the one in *Dothard,* that restricted some prison guard jobs to members of the same sex as the inmate:

> [W]e conclude that gender constitutes a BFOQ for the six [of 41] posts at issue here. . . . The plaintiffs further contend a BFOQ defense cannot be based on the privacy rights of the inmates and they correctly note that inmates' privacy rights are limited. . . . However, a person's interest in not being viewed unclothed by members of the opposite sex survives incarceration. . . . Whether or not the inmates could successfully assert their own right to privacy is immaterial to this case. We are concerned here with a considered prison policy that takes into account security, rehabilitation, and morale. . . . The record amply supports the claimed BFOQ. WCCC adopted its current policy of assigning only female ACOs to posts that raise inmate privacy or safety concerns based on the serious allegations and the ensuing problems with morale among both the inmates and the ACOs. To comply with an EEOC settlement, it conducted an extensive survey of post duties before determining which posts should be designated female-only. Each designated female-only post is residential and requires the ACO on duty to observe the inmates in the showers and toilet areas for the prison's own security or provides unsupervised access to the inmates. The state's legitimate penological interests outweigh whatever interests the male ACOs may have in standing the watches of their choice.

Page 349. Add at end of note 14:

EEOC v. HI 40 Corp., Inc., 953 F. Supp 301 (W.D. Mo. 1996) (being female was not a bona fide occupational qualification for a counselor at employer's weight loss centers, despite the centers' mostly female customers' preference for female counselors; there was no showing that the ability to take measurements and counsel customers on weight loss was a talent uniquely possessed by women, or that employing male counselors would pose any safety risk to customers or make taking body measurements and counseling inefficient).

3. *Voluntary Affirmative Action*

Page 376. Add at end of carryover Note 13:

The Supreme Court granted certiorari in *Taxman* but the parties settled the dispute prior to its being argued. Accordingly, the Court dismissed the case,

118 S. Ct. 595 (1997), thus pretermitting any definitive decision. See Michael J. Zimmer, *Taxman*, Affirmative Action Dodges Five Bullets, 1 U. Pa. J. Lab. & Emp. L. 229 (1998).

Page 376.   Add new Note 14A:

14A. In Maitland v. University of Minnesota, 155 F.3d 1013 (8th Cir. 1998), the male plaintiff challenged raises given to female employees pursuant to the settlement of their sex discrimination suit. The underlying case had involved disputed statistical models as to whether women were the victims of sex discrimination, or whether the disparities in their salaries were due to other factors. *Maitland* held that this dispute meant that there was a genuine issue as to whether the settlement was justified, that is, whether there was "a manifest or conspicuous imbalance in salaries based on gender" which the settlement was designed to address. Id. at 1018. In short, because it was not clear that there was ever a violation of Title VII as to the women who benefitted by the settlement, the male plaintiff's suit could go forward.

4.   Affirmative Action and the Constitution

Page 396.   Add new Note 2A:

2A. The remedial justification has often been argued to reach only affirmative action intended to redress prior discrimination by the state agency in question. But private discrimination in the past was endemic. Can a state actor use affirmative action to redress the consequences of such discrimination? See Ian Ayres & Frederick E. Vars, When Does Private Discrimination Justify Public Affirmative Action?, 98 Colum. L. Rev. 1577 (1998) (a majority of the Justices in *Croson* explicitly recognized private discrimination as a justification for a racial set-aside).

Page 396.   Add at the end of Note 3:

In Boston Police Super. Officers Fedn. v. City of Boston, 147 F.3d 13 (1st Cir. 1998), the court upheld a challenge to the Boston police department's bypassing of a number of white candidates on a promotion test list in order to promote an African American whose score on the test was a point lower than the white's. The compelling governmental interest was to remedy past discrimination by the police department. Looking back at a long history of discrimination, the court held that affirmative action was still necessary. While a consent decree had been entered in 1972 to remedy initial appointment discrimination, the effects of past discrimination were still present in the rank of lieutenant. The narrowly tailored test was satisfied because there was only one point difference in test scores and, within a short period, the white plaintiffs were all promoted.

Page 397.   Add at end of Note 8:

In Piscataway Township Bd. of Educ. v. Taxman, 91 F.3d 1547 (3d Cir. 1996) (en banc), *cert. dismissed*, 117 S. Ct. 2506 (1997), the court claimed to be following *Weber* and *Johnson* in upholding a Title VII challenge to a school board's decision to layoff a white teacher and keep the only African-American teacher in its high school's business education department where both were deemed exactly equally qualified. In fact, the court appeared to be importing the constitutional approach of *Croson* and *Adarand* into its interpretation of Title VII by limiting affirmative action to an employer's remediation of its own past discrimination:

> The Board admits that it did not act to remedy the effects of past employment discrimination. The parties have stipulated that neither the Board's adoption of its affirmative action policy nor its subsequent decision to apply it in choosing between Taxman and Williams was intended to remedy the results of any prior discrimination or identified underrepresentation of Blacks within the Piscataway School District's teacher workforce as a whole.

Id at 1563. Some have argued the Third Circuit's approach flies in the face of stare decisis in its strongest form. See Neal v. United States, 516 U.S. 284, 295 (1996) ("One reason that we give great weight to *stare decisis* in the area of statutory construction is that 'Congress is free to change this Court's interpretation of its legislation.'"). After *Weber* and *Johnson*, Congress did speak as to affirmative action in § 116 of the Civil Rights Act of 1991,102 Pub. L. No. 166, 105 Stat. 1071, 1079 (1991), which provides:

> Section 116. Lawful Court Ordered Remedies, Affirmative Action, and Conciliation Agreement Not Affected.
> Nothing in the amendments made by this title shall be construed to affect court-ordered remedies, affirmative action, or conciliation agreements, that are in accordance with the law.

Michael J. Zimmer, *Taxman:* Affirmative Action Dodges Five Bullets, 1 U. Pa. J. Lab. & Emp. L. 229, 235 (1998), concludes that § 116 gives "no support to justify any change in the law of voluntary affirmative action. Further, by speaking about affirmative action in § 116, Congress has gone beyond the mere 'silent or passive assent' connoted by the word 'acquiescence.' Whether or not § 116 amounts to a full reenactment of *Weber/Johnson*, it is a statement recognizing the law in those cases. Thus, under any view, § 116 bolsters *We-*

31

ber/Johnson and the stare decisis effect that the courts should give to that law." 1 U. Pa. J. Lab. & Emp. L. 229 (1998); see also Ann C. McGinley & Michael J. Yelnosky, *Board of Education v. Taxman,* 4 Roger Williams U. L. Rev. 205 (1998); Ann C. McGinley, Affirmative Action Awash in Confusion: Backward-Looking-Future Oriented Justifications for Race Conscious Measures, 4 Roger Williams U. L. Rev. 209 (1998); Michael J. Yelnosky, Whither *Weber,* 4 Roger Williams U. L. Rev. 257 (1998).

Chapter 5

Systemic Disparate Impact Discrimination

A. THE GENERAL STRUCTURE OF DISPARATE IMPACT DISCRIMINATION

Page 417.   Add new Note 13A:

13A.   Does the disparate impact theory encourage the hiring of minorities and women without regard to their qualifications? During the debates on the 1991 Amendments, opponents vociferously claimed that disparate impact would have such a result. But Ian Ayres & Peter Siegelman, The Q-Word as Red Herring: Why Disparate Impact Liability Does Not Induce Hiring Quotas, 74 Tex. L. Rev. 1487 (1996), challenge that claim. They note that prior authors, including John J. Donohue III & Peter Siegelman, The Changing Nature of Employment Discrimination Litigation, 43 Stan. L. Rev. 983, 1015-21, 1023-32 (1991), and Richard Posner, The Efficiency and the Efficacy of Title VII, 136 U. Pa. L. Rev. 513, 519 (1987), recognized tension between protecting applicants against discrimination in hiring and protecting workers from discriminatory firing after they have been hired. Antidiscrimination law forbids both kinds of conduct, but the two prohibitions are inherently at odds. By making it harder to fire certain workers, employment discrimination law tends to make these workers less attractive prospects at the hiring stage. An employer would prefer to hire someone who can be easily fired (should that prove necessary) than an otherwise identical applicant whose firing would be subject to legal scrutiny. Thus, protection against discriminatory firing acts as a kind of tax on hiring those to whom it is extended. 74 Tex. L. Rev. at 1488-89. Ayres & Siegelman then argue that, far from producing hiring quotas that induce employers to discriminate in favor of minorities, disparate impact liability may actually induce hiring discrimination against minorities (and other protected groups). Id. at 1489. This thesis rests on the claim that the Supreme Court's statistical analysis makes it easier to bring a firing case than a hiring case. By making it harder to fire protected workers, disparate impact liability discourages probationary employment generally and might even lead employers to deliberately discriminate against protected workers at the hiring stage. Id. at 1491. Does this suggest that both proponents and opponents of the 1991 Amendments were wrong in their assessments?

Page 417. Add new Note 15A:

15A. Impact analysis requires a concrete inquiry. See Brown v. Coach Stores Inc., 165 F.3d 706 (2d Cir. (1998)) (even if an employer's unlawful discrimination dissuaded plaintiff from applying for positions, she must identify the particular positions — posted or nonposted — for which she otherwise would have applied).

NOTE ON IMPACT ANALYSIS UNDER THE ADEA

Page 422. Add at top of page before "Steven Kaminshine":

Mack A. Player, Wards Cove Packing or Not Wards Cove Packing? That is Not the Question: Some Thoughts on Impact Analysis Under the Age Discrimination in Employment Act, 31 U. Rich. L. Rev. 819 (1997) (arguing in favor of impact analysis but urging a less demanding business necessity defense by focusing on "reasonable factors other than age");

Page 422. Add at end of carryover paragraph:

Keith R. Fentonmiller, The Continuing Validity of Disparate Impact Analysis for Federal-sector Age Discrimination Claims, 47 Am. U.L. Rev. 1071, 1072-73 (1998) ("the unique statutory language of section 15, combined with its legislative history and parallel to corresponding provisions of Title VII mandate the continuing application of disparate impact analysis in ADEA cases against the federal government" regardless of whether disparate impact is more generally applied under that statute).

B.   PLAINTIFF'S PRIMA FACIE CASE: PROVING THE IMPACT ELEMENT

1.   *Actual Versus Theoretical Disparate Impact*

Page 429.   Add at end of Note 3:

Cf. Newark Branch, NAACP v. City of Bayonne, 134 F.3d 113 (3d Cir. 1998) (residency requirement did not in fact have a disparate impact on African-Americans although statistics suggested it was likely to have such an impact).

2.   *Discrete Practices, Multicomponent Selection Processes, and the Bottom Line*

NOTE ON MULTIPLE-COMPONENT SYSTEMS

Page 457.   Add after last full paragraph:

In United States v. City of Warren, Michigan, 138 F.3d 1083, 1093 (6th Cir. 1998), the City had required all municipal employees to reside in the city and refused to advertise for municipal job openings outside predominately white Macomb County, a suburb of Detroit. The district court found for the city because the United States failed to introduce statistical evidence to prove that the recruitment practices had a disparate impact. The Sixth Circuit reversed:

> Because of the concurrence of the residency requirement and the challenged recruiting practices, the statistical proof which Wards Cove generally requires was unattainable in this case. . . . Wards Cove does not [however] preclude the United States' claim for failing to isolate and quantify the effects of Warren's discriminatory employment practices simply because two practices, both of which the district court has held to be unlawful [as applied to police and firefighter jobs], converged to discourage black applicants. Indeed, such a result would be anomalous and contrary to Wards Cove's explicit recognition that when, as here, certain employment practices obscure labor-market statis-

35

tics, alternative statistical analysis suffices to establish a prima facie disparate impact case.

4. Identifying Criteria Appropriate for Impact Analysis

Page 469.   Add at end of Note 5:

See also Davey v. City of Omaha, 107 F.3d 587 (8th Cir. 1997) (decision to group all employees into four salary classifications is an employment practice subject to disparate impact analysis). See Alfred W. Blumrosen, Ruth G. Blumrosen, Marco Carmigani, & Thomas Daly, Downsizing and Employee Rights, 50 Rutgers L. Rev. (1998) (argues that disparate impact analysis applies to employer decisions to downsize).

Page 469.   Add new Note 5A:

5A. Can disparate impact be used to attack policy decisions of employers such as the decision to require all employees to sign agreements to arbitrate all disputes arising out of employment? See, Miriam A. Cherry, Not-So-Arbitrary Arbitration: Using Title VII Disparate Impact Analysis to Invalidate Employment Contracts that Discriminate, 21 Harv. Women's L. J. 267 (1998). While a policy limited to arbitrating claims of, say, race discrimination could have a disparate impact on African Americans, how would a plaintiff prove impact if the policy applied to all employment disputes?

C.   DEFENDANT'S CASE: BUSINESS NECESSITY AND JOB RELATEDNESS

Page 493.   Add at end of first paragraph after extract:

Andrew C. Spiropoulos, Defining the Business Necessity Defense to the Disparate Impact Cause of Action: Finding the Golden Mean, 74 N.C. L. Rev. 1479, 1485 (1996) (arguing that the Supreme Court opinions articulated two very different versions of the business necessity defense: a strict one that would be very difficult for employers to meet, and a lenient one that would give employers more discretion; fulfilling the objectives of Title VII to remove artificial barriers to employment while preserving legitimate employer prerogatives requires establishing different standards for different types of jobs. A more flexible standard of business necessity under the 1991 Amendment should be applied to qualifications for positions that, because of their

D.   Alternative Employment Practices

difficulty, great responsibility, or special risks to the public, require skills or intangible qualities that cannot be measured empirically. In the vast majority of jobs where such qualifications are not necessary, the stricter standards of necessity should apply.).

D.   ALTERNATIVE EMPLOYMENT
PRACTICES

Page 509.   Add new Note 4:

4. For an argument, based on Justice Scalia's plain meaning approach to statutory interpretation, that § 703(k)(1)(A)(ii) creates a new right of action, independent of the basic § 703(k)(1)(A)(i) group disparate impact action, see Michael J. Zimmer, Individual Disparate Impact Law: The Plain Meaning of the 1991 Civil Rights Act, 30 Loy. U. Chi. L.J ___ (1998). Essentially, Professor Zimmer argues that § 703 (k) (1) (A) expressly recognizes two ways of establishing a disparate treatment claim. Paragraph (i) more or less codifies the traditional notion that a practice is subject to disparate impact attack if it has an unjustified impact on race, gender or other protected groups. But, because it is phrased in the disjunctive, paragraph (ii) is expressly drafted as an alternative method of establishing a violation, and does not include any requirement of proof of disparity of impact on anyone. A violation occurs if:

> (ii) the complaining party makes the demonstration described in subparagraph (c) with respect to an alternative employment practice and the respondant refuses to adopt such alternative employment practice.

This reading would have the odd result of Congress labelling something "disparate impact" without any requirement of proving any disparity of impact on any group. But requiring a showing of disparate impact under (ii) would contravene the plain meaning of the text.

If this view is taken, § 703(k)(1)(A)(ii), would create an entirely new "individual disparate impact" action. An individual protected by Title VII would be able to establish a disparate impact claim under § 703(k)(1)(A)(ii) simply by proving: (1) that the employer took adverse action based on an "employment practice," (2) that an alternative practice exists that serves the employer's interests yet would not adversely affect the plaintiff, and (3) that the employer refused to adopt the better alternative. Contrary to pre-existing Title VII law, this new cause of action neither includes an intent to discriminate or pretext element nor requires any showing of group impact. How would this new cause of action for "individual disparate impact" work for an employee who was discharged, allegedly for excessive tardiness? Aren't there many alternatives available in most workplaces that would allow for flexibility in starting times?

An advantage of joining an individual disparate impact action with one for individual disparate treatment is the interaction of the two: To the extent the employer tries to characterize its action as not being based on an employment practice, the adverse action will then appear to be ad hoc, perhaps, subjective and therefore more likely to be found to be the product of intent to discriminate. To the extent the employer claims the non-discriminatory basis for its adverse action against plaintiff is merely the application of a neutral employment policy or practice, it is conceding the first part of the §703(k)(1)(A)(ii) action. That still requires plaintiff to prove that an alternative exists that satisfies the employer's legitimate interests and that the employer refused to adopt it.

If faced with the choice of which of the two to proceed under, plaintiffs would prefer the individual disparate treatment action since it provides for the possibility of compensatory and punitive damages as well as a right to trial by jury, rights that are not available in the individual disparate impact action.

Chapter 6

Interrelation of the Disparate
Treatment and Disparate Impact
Theories of Discrimination

B. THE RELATIONSHIP BETWEEN DISPARATE IMPACT AND TREATMENT WHERE THERE IS A STATISTICAL SHOWING OF EFFECTS

NOTE ON THE RELATIONSHIP BETWEEN INDIVIDUAL AND SYSTEMIC DISPARATE TREATMENT CASES

Page 570.   Add at end of the carryover paragraph:

More recently, the Fourth Circuit ruled that individuals could not rely on the *Teamsters* method of proving systemic disparate treatment in a private, non-class action. In Lowery v. Circuit City Stores, Inc., 158 F.3d 742 (4th Cir. 1998), 11 African-American current and former employees sued individually and on behalf of all African-Americans employed at the defendant's headquarters claiming race discrimination in promotions. After initially conditionally certifying a class action, the trial court then decertified the class on grounds of fairness to the defendant and efficiency in litigating the case. Nineteen claims of the six remaining plaintiffs went to trial. Plaintiffs' case focused on the pattern or practice of the defendant. The jury found that it had engaged in a pattern or practice of racial discrimination in promotions but found in favor of only three of the individual claims. Based on this finding of a pattern or practice, the district court then imposed extensive injunctive relief. On appeal, the Fourth Circuit reversed the finding of pattern or practice liability:

> Although § 707 applies to suits brought by the government, the *Teamsters* decision implicitly endorsed the application of pattern or practice principles and rules of proof to class action lawsuits brought by private parties. . . . On the other hand, in a private, non-class action, where individual plaintiffs allege discrimination in violation of Title VII, the plaintiffs typically prove that discrimination by satisfying the shifting burden of proof scheme set forth in *McDonnell Douglas* and its progeny. . . . [W]e conclude that, although such plaintiffs may use evidence of a pattern or practice of discrimination to help prove claims of individual discrimination within the *McDonnell Douglas* framework, individual plaintiff are not entitled to the benefit of the *Teamsters* method of proof.

The court reasoned that the Supreme Court has never applied the *Teamsters* method in a private, non-class suit. Further, the main thrust of the proof in a pattern or practice action is common questions of fact, "i.e., whether the employer utilized a pattern or practice which discriminated against the class. When the class plaintiffs prove the existence of a discriminatory practice, then that finding benefits them in the adjudication of individual claims by creating a presumption that the individual class members were victims of the discriminatory practice. On the other hand, an individual plaintiff in a private, non-class action alleging employment discrimination is not litigating common questions of fact, but the discrete question of whether the employer discriminated against the plaintiff in a specific instance." Id. at 761. Doesn't this holding require the court to reverse, rather than as it did to affirm, the decision of the district court to decertify the class where that decision was based on fairness to the defendant and court efficiency? What about the goals of eradicating discrimination and fairness to plaintiffs?

The Fourth Circuit did list the ways in which pattern or practice evidence may be used in an individual disparate treatment action.

> Evidence of a pattern or practice of discrimination may very well be useful and relevant to prove the fourth element of a [*McDonnell Douglas*] prima facie case, that the individual's adverse employment action occurred under circumstances giving rise to an inference of unlawful discrimination, or that the employer's articulated reasons for the adverse action was [sic] merely pretext, or to

A. The Relationship Between Disparate Impact and Treatment

> establish the plaintiff's ultimate burden. However, statistics alone cannot establish a prima facie case of individual disparate treatment, for all four elements of a prima facie case must be established.

Id. While the Supreme Court may not have so far decided a private, non-class suit by relying on *Teamsters,* has the Court decided that all plaintiffs claiming individual disparate treatment must meet *McDonnell Douglas?* What about *Price Waterhouse?*

Chapter 7

Special Problems in Applying
Title VII, Section 1981,
and the ADEA

B. COVERAGE OF TITLE VII, SECTION 1981, AND THE ADEA

Page 587. Add at end of carryover paragraph:

Recent appellate decisions have emphasized the factors associated with the hybrid test, although sometimes purporting to apply either the common law or economic realities test. E.g., EEOC v. North Knox Sch. Corp., 154 F.3d 744 (7th Cir. 1998); Cilecek v. Inova Health Sys. Services, 115 F.3d 256 (4th Cir. 1997); Speen v. Crown Clothing Corp., 102 F.3d 625 (1st Cir. 1996), *cert. denied*, 520 U.S. 1276 (1997); Simpson v. Ernst & Young, 100 F.3d 436 (6th Cir. 1996); *cert. denied*, 520 U.S. 1248 (1997).

Page 588. Add at end of carryover paragraph:

Recent cases have divided over whether § 1981 encompasses at-will employment. Some cases indicate that coverage depends upon whether state law regards at-will employment as a contractual relationship. The cases are collected in Fadeyi v. Planned Parenthood Assn., 160 F.3d 1048 (5th Cir. 1998). The *Fadeyi* court, relying on inferences drawn from Supreme Court precedents and § 1981's legislative history, concluded that Congress intended § 1981 to protect at-will employees regardless of state law. Nevertheless, the court went on to determine that at-will employment is a contractual relationship under Texas law. In contrast to *Fadeyi*, another recent decision held that § 1981 does not apply to at-will employment, apparently assuming that New York does not regard such employment as a contractual relationship. Moorer v. Grumman Aerospace Corp., 964 F. Supp. 665 (E.D.N.Y. 1997), *aff'd on grounds stated below*, 162 F.3d 1148 (2d Cir. 1998).

Page 589. Add before last sentence in Note 8:

Similarly, apparent employees who are actually independent contractors are not counted. Ost v. West Suburban Travelers Limousine, Inc., 88 F.3d 435 (7th Cir. 1996) (limousine drivers).

Page 589. Add to Note 8 after "E.g." in the third-to-last line:

Sharpe v. Jefferson Distrib. Co., 148 F.3d 676 (7th Cir. 1998);

Page 589. Add at end of Note 8:

When a foreign corporation has an office in the United States, the courts are divided on whether the corporation's foreign employees are counted. Morelli v. Cedel, 141 F.3d 39 (2d Cir. 1996), and the cases cited there. A similar problem is whether one counts only the employees of an instrumentality of a state or political subdivision or all the employees of the state or political subdivision. Palmer v. Arkansas Council on Econ. Educ., 154 F.3d 892 (8th Cir. 1998), and cases cited there.

Page 590. Add at end of Note 11:

Section 1981 does not apply to federal employment. Lee v. Hughes, 145 F.3d 1272 (11th Cir. 1998).

Page 591. Add in carryover Note 13 after the citation to **Diggs:**

Accord, Bender v. Suburban Hosp., 159 F.3d 186 (4th Cir. 1998); Alexander v. Rush N. Shore Med. Ctr., 101 F.3d 487 (7th Cir. 1996).

Page 592.   Add at end of carryover Note 15:

The Fourth Circuit has held that Title VII (and presumably the other anti-discrimination statutes) does not protect an alien who is discriminatorily denied employment when the alien cannot lawfully work in the United States. Egbuna v. Time-Life Libraries, Inc., 153 F.3d 184 (4th Cir. 1998) (en banc). The court relied on the Immigration Reform and Control Act of 1986, see pp. 787-91, which outlaws such employment. The court's reasoning suggests, however, that Title VII may be applicable to at least some post-hiring discrimination against such aliens.

Page 593.   Add at end of carryover Note 16:

A provision in the ADEA, when read literally, permits an "uncontrolled" foreign corporation to discriminate in its employment both in and outside the United States, § 4(h)(2), 29 U.S.C.A. § 623(h)(2). But the Second Circuit has held that the provision was not intended to include employment within the United States. Morelli v. Cedel, 141 F.3d 39 (2d Cir. 1998).

C.   GENDER DISCRIMINATION

1.   Pregnancy

Page 597.   Add at end of carryover Note 1:

The Seventh Circuit in Marshall v. American Hospital Assn., 157 F.3d 520 (7th Cir. 1998) also found it permissible for an employer to take pregnancy leave into account in making employment decisions. In *Marshall*, the plaintiff's pregnancy leave was scheduled during the busiest time of the year prior to an important annual conference. The court found that the plaintiff presented no evidence that a non-pregnant probationary employee who required extended leave in the months immediately preceding the annual conference would not have been terminated.

Page 598.   Add at end of Note 7:

See In re Carnegie Cntr. Associates, 129 F.3d 290 (3d Cir. 1997) (employer may consider the fact that an employee is on pregnancy leave when making layoff decisions if individuals on temporary disability leave are treated the same way)

Page 599.   Add new Notes 11 through 13:

11. The Fifth and Sixth Circuits disagree on the appropriate comparison to be made in pregnancy discrimination cases. The Sixth Circuit held that pregnancy discrimination is established if the pregnant employee is treated differently than a non-pregnant employee who is similarly situated solely with respect to that employee's ability or inability to work. Applying this theory, the court found that the employer could violate the statute by denying light duty to a pregnant employee on the ground that her work limitation, unlike the work limitations of accommodated employees, was not due to a job-related injury. According to the court, the pregnant employee must be treated the same as other workers with similar work limitations regardless of the source of the limitation. Ensley-Gaines v. Runyon, 100 F.3d 1220 (6th Cir. 1996). The Fifth Circuit disagreed, finding no discrimination under similar circumstances on the ground that the pregnant employee was treated the same as other employees with similar work restrictions whose injuries or illnesses were not employment related. Urbano v. Continental Airlines, 138 F.3d 204 (5th Cir. 1998).

12. Can a plaintiff establish pregnancy discrimination by demonstrating that she has been treated less favorably than other pregnant workers? The Eighth Circuit allowed a plaintiff to establish liability on the basis of such evidence. The plaintiff, unlike the other pregnant employees, suffered from pregnancy related complications. See Deneen v. Northwest Airlines, 132 F.3d 431 (8th Cir. 1998).

13. Is it a form of pregnancy discrimination to require clerical employees to submit to pregnancy tests in a pre-employment physical? See Norman-Bloodsaw v. Lawrence Berkeley Lab., 135 F.3d 1260 (9th Cir. 1998) (yes).

Page 602.   Add new Note 7:

7. Ilhardt v. Sara Lee Corp., 118 F.3d 1151 (7th Cir. 1997) raises another lack of comparison issue that seems to implicate gender. In *Ilhardt*, a female associate began working part-time after the birth of her first child. Several years later while in her third pregnancy, the associate was laid off. The reason given was her part-time status. Because there were no other part-time associates, it was not possible to make a comparison to establish disparate treatment. The court found insufficient evidence of disparate impact even though the associate pointed to studies indicating that most part-time employees are women with child care responsibilities. The court found the studies, which

were conducted in the 1970's and 1980's, unpersuasive because they were outdated.

Page 613.   Add at end of the first full paragraph:

One district court concluded that, although normal pregnancies are not covered under the ADA, complications or conditions arising out of pregnancy may be covered. Pregnancy related symptoms cited by the court as possible bases for an ADA claim included severe back pain, morning sickness, leaking or discharge, and dizziness. See Cerrato v. Durham, 941 F. Supp 388 (S.D.N.Y. 1996).

Does the ADA suggest a different approach to pregnancy discrimination? Pamela S. Karlan & George Rutherglen, Disabilities, Discrimination, and Reasonable Accommodation, 46 Duke L.J. 1, 47-48 (1996):

> The broader implications of the duty of reasonable accommodation result from its departure from the concept of discrimination as ordinarily understood. The duty does not presuppose a finding of prior discrimination [or], a general affirmative action plan. . . . If the duty of reasonable accommodation succeeds for the disabled, it suggests considering a similar model for members of other protected classes. Perhaps an open-ended responsibility to enable all workers to enjoy equal employment opportunities by taking account of the particular way in which their membership in a protected class has impaired their full participation in the economy would do more to end the continuing effects of past discrimination than the current combination of broad negative prohibitions and bureaucratic class-wide preferences.

Page 614.   Insert before "Note on Related Medical Conditions":

The Sixth Circuit's interpretation of the PDA, which requires pregnant women to be treated the same as employees similar in their ability or inability to work, regardless of the source of the limiting condition, would seemingly allow pregnancy discrimination claims based on a comparison with the treatment of individuals protected by the ADA. The argument would be that the PDA requires employers to treat individuals with similar work limitations the same way — the temporary or permanent nature of the limitation would be irrelevant. See Ensley-Gaines v. Runyon, supra, Supplement p. 46. In contrast, the Fifth Circuit would find no violation as long as some other similarly limited employee was treated in the same way — for example, an employee with an injury not qualifying as a disability under the ADA. See Urbano v. Continental Airlines, supra, Supplement p. 46.

Page 615.   Add at end of the carryover paragraph:

In Piantanida v. Wyman Cntr., Inc., 116 F.3d 340 (8th Cir. 1997) the Eighth Circuit decided that discrimination on the basis of being a "new mother" is not cognizable under the PDA. Even if child care is not a related medical condition under the PDA, wouldn't a decision based on "new mother" status be sex discrimination if it is based on stereotypes about exclusive female responsibility for child care?

Page 615.   Add at end of the first full paragraph:

Connecticut, New York, and Texas have laws protecting a mother's right to breast-feed. See 1997 Ct. Gen. Stat. Ann. 46a-64 (West 1998) (prohibiting public accommodations, resorts, and amusements from restricting or limiting a mother's right to breast-feed her child); NY Civ. Rights Law § 79-e (McKinney 1998) (guaranteeing mothers the right to breast-feed their babies "in any location, public or private, where the mother is otherwise authorized to be"); Tex. Health & Safety Code Ann. § 165.002 (West 1998) (same).

Page 616.   Add at end of the third full paragraph:

The Eighth Circuit has held that excluding coverage for female infertility problems does not violate the PDA because infertility is not pregnancy, childbirth, or a related medical condition and because the employer's policy was gender-neutral. Krauel v. Iowa Methodist Med. Cntr. 45 F.3d 674, 680 (8th Cir. 1996). The court reached this decision in spite of evidence indicating that the employer's vice president had told the plaintiff "that the Plan excluded coverage for infertility treatment coverage because too many women of child-bearing age were employed by IMMC and infertility treatments result in too many multiple births, thereby creating a financial burden on the Plan." Id. at 680. The court decided that having concluded that infertility is not pregnancy, childbirth, or a related medical condition, the VP's comments were not probative of discrimination on any prohibited basis. Do you agree? Is a hysterectomy a related medical condition under the PDA? See Williams v. MacFrugal's Bargains, 67 Cal. App. 4th 479 (1998) (no, applying language identical to the PDA under California's Fair Employment and Housing Act).

Page 626.   Add at end of carryover Note 8:

See also Sanders v. Casa View Baptist Church, 134 F.3d 331 (5th Cir. 1998) (summary judgment in favor of employer affirmed the termination of two

C. Gender Discrimination

female employees because their employer's disapproval of adultery was not gender discrimination).

2. Sexual Harassment

Page 627.   Add after the first full paragraph:

One issue that arises in quid pro quo harassment cases is whether the adverse consequences the plaintiff alleges are significant enough to make out a quid pro quo case rather than merely a hostile environment harassment claim. Plaintiffs may wish to characterize their claims as quid pro quo to avoid the many issues that arise in hostile environment cases, including the need to establish that the harassment was severe and pervasive in order to prevail. The Seventh Circuit has held that a series of minimal adverse consequences for refusing a supervisor's sexual advances can be cumulated to show the tangible job detriment necessary to support a quid pro quo sexual harassment claim. See Bryson v. Chicago State Univ., 96 F.3d 912 (7th Cir. 1996) (tenured university professor who lost title of Special Assistant to the Dean and was denied reappointment to prestigious committees stated a claim of quid pro quo harassment because adverse actions interfered with the administrative career track she was seeking).

Page 633.   Add at end of Note 2:

In Nichols v. American Natl. Ins. Co., 154 F.3d 875 (8th Cir. 1998), the Eighth Circuit reversed a jury verdict against a plaintiff who alleged that she was subjected to a hostile environment at work that included physical assaults. The district court erred by admitting psychiatric testimony impugning the plaintiff's credibility that was not a proper subject for expert psychiatric testimony. In addition, the district court erred by admitting evidence that the plaintiff had undergone an abortion inconsistent with her religious beliefs. The Eighth Circuit ruled that this testimony was highly prejudicial and of little probative value.

Page 633.   Add at end of Note 5:

Plaintiffs seeking emotional distress damages may need to present psychiatric testimony in order to prevail. See Patterson v. P.H.P. Healthcare, 90 F.3d 927 (5th Cir. 1996) (unlawfully discharged black employee's testimony about his emotional response to being referred to as "porch monkey" or "nigger" does not support more than nominal damages absent corroborating expert medical or psychological evidence of sleeplessness, anxiety, or depression).

Page 634–638.   Delete "Note on Proving that Harassment Is Gender Based."

Page 639.   Add to end of first full paragraph:

In Analogizing Race and Sex in Workplace Harassment Claims, 58 Ohio St. L.J. 819 (1997), Professor L. Camille Hébert, while recognizing some benefits to analogizing race and sex harassment, cautions of dangers:

> [S]ome courts have used explicit and implicit analogies between race and sex to make it more difficult to establish the existence of racial harassment, by importing the standards for sexual harassment into the standards of proof for racial harassment claims. Accordingly, some courts have begun to use language suggesting that "welcomeness" may be an issue in racial harassment claims, so that it becomes relevant to ask whether the target of harassment somehow invited that behavior. The movement of courts toward a more "gender-neutral" . . . perspective for judging sexually harassing conduct may also cause courts to reject the relevance of the experience of racial minorities with racially threatening and offensive conduct. The use of the standard developed in the context of sexual harassment requiring that conduct be "severe or pervasive" in order to be actionable has led the courts to conclude that even quite damaging and serious racially motivated behavior, including references to lynching or racially motivated assault, is insufficient to state a cause of action for racial harassment. The use of standards of employer liability developed in connection with sexual harassment claims in the context of racial harassment claims may well leave many employees victimized by racially hostile workplaces and no remedy for this discriminatory and damaging behavior. Analogies between race and sex may also lead courts to conclude that even racially explicit conduct is not racially motivated, similar to the conclusions drawn by some courts that sexually explicit conduct is not motivated by gender.

Id. at 878-879.

Page 644.   Add new Note 1A:

1A. The Second Circuit has held that judges should be cautious in granting summary judgment in sexual harassment cases because juries are better qualified to evaluate appropriate behavior in the workplace:

> Today, while gender relations in the workplace are rapidly evolving, and views of what is appropriate behavior are diverse and shifting, a jury made up of a

cross-section of our heterogenous communities provides the appropriate institution for deciding whether borderline situations should be characterized as
sexual harassment. . . .

Gallagher v. Delaney, 139 F.3d 338, 342 (2d Cir. 1998). Is this a good solution to the problem of defining actionable sexual harassment? Are decisions
by juries capable of setting new standards of behavior? Consider the following remarks in another Second Circuit case:

> . . . American popular culture can, on occasion, be highly sexist and offensive.
> What *is*, is not always what is right, and reasonable people can take justifiable
> offense at comments that the vulgar among us, even if they are a majority,
> would consider acceptable.

Torres v. Pisano, 116 F.3d 625, 633 n.7 (2d Cir. 1997). If those who believe
vulgar comments are acceptable constitute a majority of the population, how
can juries be expected to improve sexist behavior in the workplace?

Page 645.   Add new Note 3A:

3A. After *Harris*, courts continue to disagree about the showing that a
plaintiff must make to establish that she was subjected to a hostile work environment. The Sixth Circuit requires plaintiffs to demonstrate that the harassment "had the effect of unreasonably interfering with the plaintiff's work
performance and creating an intimidating, hostile, or offensive working environment. . . ." Harrison v. Metropolitan Govt. of Nashville, 80 F.3d 1107,
1118 (6th Cir. 1996) (racial harassment case quoting Rabidue v. Osceola
Refining Co., 805 F.2d 611, 619 (6th Cir. 1986)). The Tenth Circuit, in contrast, has held that a woman who continues to enjoy her work and intends to
stay on the job can, nonetheless, establish that she has been a victim of hostile environment harassment. Davis v. United States Postal Serv., 142 F.3d
1334 (10th Cir. 1998). Under this standard a sexual harassment claimant is
"not required to prove that her tangible productivity or work performance declined or that her ability to do her job was impaired." Smith v. Norwest Fin.
Acceptance, 129 F.3d 1408, 1413 (10th Cir. 1997).

Page 645.   Add at end of Note 5:

Courts have resisted finding actionable harassment based on offensive comments. See, e.g., Skouby v. Prudential Ins. Co. of Am., 130 F.3d 794 (7th Cir.
1997) (male employees' banter about attending striptease club and presenta-
tion to plaintiff of eight to ten drawings with sexual themes not severe or

pervasive); Sprague v. Thorn Americas, Inc., 129 F.3d 1355 (10th Cir. 1997) (sporadic comments over 16-month period did not create a hostile environment; comments included joking request to undo her top button, reference to PMS, staring down her dress and joking about it, and referring to a jewelry item as "kinky"); Black v. Zaring Homes, 104 F.3d 822 (6th Cir. 1997) (numerous comments at real estate meetings referring to property adjacent to Hooters Restaurant as "Titsville" or "Twin Peaks" and joking about client named "Busam" and about whether plaintiff was seen dancing on the tables at a nearby biker bar insufficient to create a hostile environment).

Courts have been more open to finding a hostile environment based on verbal harassment when the comments are alleged to be "commonplace," "ongoing," and "continuing" over a long period of time. See Abeita v. TransAmerica Mailings, 159 F.3d 246 (6th Cir. 1998). Allegations that verbal harassment occurred in a public setting in a small office convinced the court to find actionable harassment. In *Abeita* a male supervisor told the plaintiff that she should "get a little this weekend" so she would "come back in a better mood." He also told her she "must be a sad piece of ass" who "can't keep a man."

Page 645. *Add at end of Note 7:*

In the highly publicized case of Jones v. Clinton, 990 F. Supp. 657 (E.D. Ark. 1998), the district court granted summary judgement, concluding that the single incident of harassment alleged by the plaintiff, although "boorish and offensive" was not sufficiently severe to constitute sexual harassment. Although the case was pursued under the equal protection clause, the court applied standards developed under Title VII. Jones alleged that then Governor Clinton invited her to his hotel room, exposed himself to her, and requested her to perform oral sex. Jones asserted that she in no way invited this behavior.

Some courts have been willing to find serious single incidents of harassment sufficient to establish liability under Title VII, especially if the complaint involves physical contact. See Taylor v. National Group, 872 F. Supp. 462 (N.D. Ohio, 1994) (female employee claimed that the president of the company struck her on the buttocks with a board); Lockard v. Pizza Hut, 162 F.3d 1062 (10th Cir. 1998) (single incident in which customer grabbed plaintiff's hair and breast was severe enough to create an actionable hostile work environment).

Courts have been reluctant to find actionable harassment for single incidents of *verbal* harassment, even in cases involving seriously offensive comments. See, e.g., Gross v. Burggraf Constr. Co., 53 F.3d 1531, 1542 (10th Cir. 1995) (isolated instance in which perpetrator stated "sometimes don't you just want to smash a woman in the face" did not establish hostile work environment claim); EEOC v. Champion Intl. Corp., 1995 U.S. Dist. LEXIS 11808 (N.D. Ill. Aug. 1, 1995) (single incident in which employee exposed himself to plaintiff and said "suck my dick, you black bitch" did not create hostile environment); Bennett v. New York City Dept. of Corrections, 705 F. Supp. 979, 983 (S.D.N.Y. 1989) (single incident in which white male corrections officer yelled at black female officer "hey black bitch, open the . . . gate" is insufficient to create a racially hostile work environment); Triplett v. Runyon, 977 F. Supp. 873 (N.D. Ill 1977). This reluctance is consistent with courts' unwillingness to find actionable harassment based solely on offensive verbal harassment. Are these cases correctly decided?

In contrast, the Seventh Circuit in Daniels v. Essex Group, Inc., 937 F.2d 1264 (7th Cir. 1991) suggested facts that could constitute racial harassment in a single incident even in the absence of physical contact:

> The Ku Klux Klan's effect on blacks calls to mind the example of a case in which only one isolated instance of harassment would be enough to establish the existence of a hostile work environment. If a black worker's colleagues came to work wearing the white hoods and robes of the Klan and proceeded to hold a cross-burning on the premises, all with the knowledge of the employer, this single incident would doubtless give rise to the employer's liability for racial harassment under Title VII.

Id. at 1274, note 4.

State courts have proven more willing than federal courts to find actionable harassment based on a single serious incident of verbal harassment. See, e.g., Bowman v. Heller, 651 N.E.2d 369 (Mass. 1995) (state law violated by male employee who superimposed female employee's face and name over pictures of nude female bodies and distributed copies of the pictures in the workplace); Nadeau v. Rainbow Rugs, 675 A.2d 973 (Me. 1996) (company president created hostile environment by offering to pay for sex with female employee); Taylor v. Metzger, 706 A.2d 685 (N.J. 1998) (County Sheriff referring to black female officer as a "jungle bunny" may establish racial harassment in violation of New Jersey law).

Page 646.   Add new Notes 11 and 12:

11. If a male (or white) employee finds it objectionable to work in an environment in which supervisors or co-workers are making discriminatory remarks about women (or African Americans), is the employee protected by Title VII? An equally divided Fourth Circuit opinion affirmed a district court ruling that white male police officers have no standing to sue under Title VII to complain about their supervisor's disparaging remarks about female and black officers. Is this decision correct? Cf. Trafficante v. Metropolitan Life Ins. Co., 409 US. 205 (1972) (in a housing discrimination case, white tenants who complain about a landlord's exclusion of black housing applicants are "person[s] aggrieved" under Title VIII).

In another case, the Eleventh Circuit held that a white employee's complaint about a co-worker's racial slurs is not protected opposition activity. Until the employer is aware of the co-worker's conduct, the slurs cannot be attributed to the employer and there is no discriminatory practice to oppose. See Little v. United Techs., 103 F.3d 956 (11th Cir. 1997) Is this decision correct?

12. Should it be possible to pursue a pattern and practice or class action case of hostile environment sexual harassment? What problems do you see? How should a court deal with the subjective aspect of a harassment claim in a class action context? See EEOC v. Mitsubishi Motor MFG., 990 F. Supp. 1059 (C.D. Ill. 1998) (allowing a pattern and practice sexual harassment action); Jenson v. Eveleth Taconite Co., 824 F. Supp. 847 (D. Minn. 1993) (finding class-wide liability for sexual harassment).

Page 646.   Add the following principal case and new Notes 1 through 12 before Ellison v. Brady:

ONCALE V. SUNDOWNER OFFSHORE SERVICES, INC.
523 U.S. 75 (1998)

Justice SCALIA delivered the opinion of the Court.

This case presents the question whether workplace harassment can violate Title VII's prohibition against "discrimination . . . because of . . . sex," when the harasser and the harassed employee are of the same sex.

I

The District Court having granted summary judgment for respondent, we must assume the facts to be as alleged by petitioner Joseph Oncale. The precise details are irrelevant to the legal point we must decide, and in the interest of both brevity and dignity we shall describe them only generally. In late October 1991, Oncale was working for respondent Sundowner Offshore Services on a Chevron U.S.A., Inc., oil platform in the Gulf of Mexico. He was employed as a roustabout on an eight-man crew which included respondents John Lyons, Danny Pippen, and Brandon Johnson. Lyons, the crane operator, and Pippen, the driller, had supervisory authority. On several occasions, Oncale was forcibly subjected to sex-related, humiliating actions against him by Lyons, Pippen and Johnson in the presence of the rest of the crew. Pippen and Lyons also physically assaulted Oncale in a sexual manner, and Lyons threatened him with rape.

Oncale's complaints to supervisory personnel produced no remedial action; in fact, the company's Safety Compliance Clerk, Valent Hohen, told

C. Gender Discrimination

Oncale that Lyons and Pippen "picked [on] him all the time too," and called him a name suggesting homosexuality. Oncale eventually quit — asking that his pink slip reflect that he "voluntarily left due to sexual harassment and verbal abuse." When asked at his deposition why he left Sundowner, Oncale stated "I felt that if I didn't leave my job, that I would be raped or forced to have sex."

[The district court held that "Mr. Oncale, a male, has no cause of action under Title VII for harassment by male co-workers." The Fifth Circuit affirmed.]

II

Title VII of the Civil Rights Act of 1964 provides, in relevant part, that "it shall be an unlawful employment practice for an employer . . . to discriminate against any individual with respect to his compensation, terms, conditions, or privileges of employment, because of such individual's race, color, religion, sex, or national origin." We have held that this not only covers "terms" and "conditions" in the narrow contractual sense, but "evinces a congressional intent to strike at the entire spectrum of disparate treatment of men and women in employment." *Meritor.* "When the workplace is permeated with discriminatory intimidation, ridicule, and insult that is sufficiently severe or pervasive to alter the conditions of the victim's employment and create an abusive working environment, Title VII is violated." *Harris.*

Title VII's prohibition of discrimination "because of . . . sex" protects men as well as women, *Newport News,* and in the related context of racial discrimination in the workplace we have rejected any conclusive presumption that an employer will not discriminate against members of his own race. "Because of the many facets of human motivation, it would be unwise to presume as a matter of law that human beings of one definable group will not discriminate against other members of that group." Castaneda v. Partida, 430 U.S. 482 (1977). In Johnson v. Transportation Agency, Santa Clara County, a male employee claimed that his employer discriminated against him because of his sex when it preferred a female employee for promotion. Although we ultimately rejected the claim on other grounds, we did not consider it significant that the supervisor who made that decision was also a man. If our precedents leave any doubt on the question, we hold today that nothing in Title VII necessarily bars a claim of discrimination "because of . . . sex" merely because the plaintiff and the defendant (or the person charged with acting on behalf of the defendant) are of the same sex.

Courts have had little trouble with that principle in cases like *Johnson,* where an employee claims to have been passed over for a job or promotion. But when the issue arises in the context of a "hostile environment" sexual harassment claim, the state and federal courts have taken a bewildering variety of stances. Some, like the Fifth Circuit in this case, have held that same-sex sexual harassment claims are never cognizable under Title VII. Other decisions say that such claims are actionable only if the plaintiff can prove that the harasser is homosexual (and thus presumably motivated by sexual desire). Compare McWilliams v. Fairfax County Board of Supervisors, 72 F.3d 1191 (4th Cir. 1996), with Wrightson v. Pizza Hut of America, 99 F.3d 138 (4th Cir. 1996). Still others suggest that workplace harassment that is sexual in content is always actionable, regardless of the harasser's sex, sexual orientation, or motivations. See Doe v. Belleville, 119 F.3d 563 (7th Cir. 1997).

We see no justification in the statutory language or our precedents for a categorical rule excluding same-sex harassment claims from the coverage of Title VII. As some courts have observed, male-on-male sexual harassment in the workplace was assuredly not the principal evil Congress was concerned with when it enacted Title VII. But statutory prohibitions often go beyond the principal evil to cover reasonably comparable evils, and it is ultimately the provisions of our laws rather than the principal concerns of our legislators by which we are governed. Title VII prohibits "discrimination . . . because of . . . sex" in the "terms" or "conditions" of employment. Our holding that this includes sexual harassment must extend to sexual harassment of any kind that meets the statutory requirements.

Respondents and their amici contend that recognizing liability for same-sex harassment will transform Title VII into a general civility code for the American workplace. But that risk is no greater for same-sex than for opposite-sex harassment, and is adequately met by careful attention to the requirements of the statute. Title VII does not prohibit all verbal or physical harassment in the workplace; it is directed only at "discrimination . . . because of . . . sex." We have never held that workplace harassment, even harassment between men and women, is automatically discrimination because of sex merely because the words used have sexual content or connotations. "The critical issue, Title VII's text indicates, is whether members of one sex are exposed to disadvantageous terms or conditions of employment to which members of the other sex are not exposed." *Harris*.

Courts and juries have found the inference of discrimination easy to draw in most male-female sexual harassment situations, because the challenged conduct typically involves explicit or implicit proposals of sexual activity; it is reasonable to assume those proposals would not have been made to someone of the same sex. The same chain of inference would be available to a plaintiff alleging same-sex harassment, if there were credible evidence that the harasser was homosexual. But harassing conduct need not be motivated by sexual desire to support an inference of discrimination on the basis of sex. A trier of fact might reasonably find such discrimination, for example, if a female victim is harassed in such sex-specific and derogatory terms by another woman as to make it clear that the harasser is motivated by general hostility to the presence of women in the workplace. A same-sex harassment plaintiff may also, of course, offer direct comparative evidence about how the alleged harasser treated members of both sexes in a mixed-sex workplace. Whatever evidentiary route the plaintiff chooses to follow, he or she must always prove that the conduct at issue was not merely tinged with offensive sexual connotations, but actually constituted "discrimination . . . because of . . . sex."

And there is another requirement that prevents Title VII from expanding into a general civility code: As we emphasized in *Meritor* and *Harris*, the statute does not reach genuine but innocuous differences in the ways men and women routinely interact with members of the same sex and of the opposite sex. The prohibition of harassment on the basis of sex requires neither asexuality nor androgyny in the workplace; it forbids only behavior so objectively offensive as to alter the "conditions" of the victim's employment. "Conduct that is not severe or pervasive enough to create an objectively hostile or abusive work environment — an environment that a reasonable person would find hostile or abusive — is beyond Title VII's purview." *Harris*.

We have always regarded that requirement as crucial, and as sufficient to ensure that courts and juries do not mistake ordinary socializing in the workplace — such as male-on-male horseplay or intersexual flirtation — for discriminatory "conditions of employment."

We have emphasized, moreover, that the objective severity of harassment should be judged from the perspective of a reasonable person in the plaintiff's position, considering "all the circumstances." *Harris*. In same-sex (as in all) harassment cases, that inquiry requires careful consideration of the social context in which particular behavior occurs and is experienced by its target. A professional football player's working environment is not severely or pervasively abusive, for example, if the coach smacks him on the buttocks as he heads onto the field-even if the same behavior would reasonably be experienced as abusive by the coach's secretary (male or female) back at the office. The real social impact of workplace behavior often depends on a constellation of surrounding circumstances, expectations, and relationships which are not fully captured by a simple recitation of the words used or the physical acts performed. Common sense, and an appropriate sensitivity to social context, will enable courts and juries to distinguish between simple teasing or roughhousing among members of the same sex, and conduct which a reasonable person in the plaintiff's position would find severely hostile or abusive. . . .

NOTES

1. In recognizing sexual harassment as a claim under Title VII, the *Meritor* Court implicitly based its theory on the heterosexual assumption that a male supervisor making sexual advances to a female employee did so because of her female gender. When a female supervisor makes sexual advances toward a male employee, the heterosexual assumption leads to the same conclusion: the conduct was gender based. When, however, plaintiffs' allegations go beyond these paradigm sexual harassment cases, proving the gender basis

of the harasser's conduct becomes more problematic. *Oncale* makes clear that, regardless of the gender of the harasser and victim, the central issue for purposes of establishing liability under Title VII is whether the terms and conditions of the victim's employment were altered because of or on the basis of sex.

2. Although *Oncale* establishes that same-sex harassment is actionable under Title VII, the question remains, when is harassment because of or on the basis of sex? The Court confirms prior opinions in which an inference of sex-based discrimination was derived from the fact that sexual advances were made by a heterosexual towards a victim of the opposite sex. Consistent with this logic, the Court indicates that sexual advances by a homosexual toward an individual of the same sex also may give rise to the inference that such action is "because of sex." Katherine M. Franke, What's Wrong With Sexual Harassment?, 49 Stan. L. Rev. 691, 732 (1997), views this as a kind of "but for" causation argument:

> To regard sexual harassment as a form of sex discrimination because the harasser would not have undertaken the conduct "but for" the sex of the victim is to understand the harasser to have engaged in sexual harassment primarily because he finds the target physically attractive, would like to have sex with her or him, and/or derives libidinous pleasure from sexualizing their otherwise professional relationship. Interestingly enough, on this view, the harasser's sexual orientation, either assumed or proven, plays a central role in determining whether the offending sexual conduct was "because of sex." In fact, in these cases "but for" causation collapses into sexual orientation. Under this view, a harasser only sexually harasses members of the class of people that he or she sexually desires. As such, "because of sex," primarily means "because of the harasser's sexual orientation," and only secondarily means "because of the victim's sex."
>
> Many same-sex harassment cases make this aspect of sexual harassment jurisprudence abundantly clear. While proof of the harasser's heterosexuality is never required in different-sex cases because it is merely assumed, proof of homosexuality is frequently required in same-sex cases in order to demonstrate that the conduct was undertaken "because of sex."

What Franke characterizes as the "homosexuals-only" rule has presumably been rejected by *Oncale*. Certainly, harassment by gays seeking sexual gratification from members of their own sex will fall within Title VII's prohibitions. Thus, plaintiffs may prevail by pleading and proving that defendant's conduct stemmed from his sexual proclivities, but the "heterosexual assumption" may mean that specific pleading will not be necessary where the plaintiff and defendant are of different sexes but will be required when the two are of the same sex. But see Ramona L. Paetzold, Same-Sex Harassment: Can It Be Sex-Related for Purposes of Title VII?, 1 Employee Rts. & Employment Policy J. 25, 52 (1997). ("if the link between sexual conduct and conduct based on sex is to be presumed for male-female cases, then it should be presumed for same-sex cases, without proof of homosexual orientation on the part of the harasser").

3. *Oncale*, however, clearly envisions the prohibition sweeping more broadly than sexual advances. What about facts such as those presented in *Oncale* itself? On remand, what evidence would you present to establish that Oncale's co-workers were harassing him based on his sex? What evidence would you present on behalf of the employer to prove an alternative motivation such as jealousy or dislike?

4. Katherine M. Franke, What's Wrong With Sexual Harassment?, 49 Stan. L. Rev. 691, 697-98 (1997), categorizes the same-sex cases which arose before *Oncale* as involving three distinct situations:

> The first set of cases involve [sic] a gay male supervisor who seeks sexual favors from or creates a sexually hostile environment for his male subordinates or coworkers. . . .
>
> The second set of cases involve [sic] nongay same-sex harassment. Here, the defendant is either heterosexual, or at least not alleged to be gay, and is charged with exhibiting sexual behavior in the workplace in such a way that another male employee regards as both unwelcome and offensive. In these cases, the harasser neither wants to have sex with the plaintiff, nor does he desire to have sex with members of the class of people to which the plaintiff belongs. Rather than sexually objectifying the plaintiff, the harasser engages in sexual behavior that is designed to or has the effect of making the plaintiff annoyed, uncomfortable, offended, humiliated, intimidated, or otherwise victimized by the defendant's conduct.
>
> The third set of same-sex sexual harassment cases are [sic] similar to those just described but differ from them in one significant way: the harassing conduct of a sexual nature was undertaken because of the plaintiff's gender identity. That is, the plaintiff was not sufficiently masculine according to the individual defendant's standards of proper masculine presentation, the gender rules of the particular workplace, or according to masculine gender normativity as defined by the culture more generally.

The first set of cases presumably easily falls within *Oncale*, if only because of what Franke describes as the "but for" argument. But after *Oncale*, what is the appropriate response to the second and third situations? Professor Franke recognizes that the second set is harder for the courts to recognize as "sex" discrimination. Would Justice Scalia? See Charles R. Calleros, Same-Sex Harassment, Textualism, Free Speech and *Oncale*: Laying the Groundwork for a Coherent and Constitutional Theory of Sexual Harassment Liability, 7 Geo. Mason L. Rev. 1, 13 (1998) (reading *Oncale* to suggest that the nature of the harassment might be gender discrimination even in a workplace with only one sex represented). As to the third set of cases, "by and large, courts have been unwilling to recognize this kind of sexual harassment — between men as a way of policing hetero-masculine gender norms — as a form of discrimination because of sex and therefore actionable as sex discrimination." 49 Stan. L. Rev. at 698. She argues "it would be both a theoretical and a descriptive mistake to characterize offensive workplace sexual conduct primarily as the expression of sexual desire. Rather, sexual harassment is best understood as the expression, in sexual terms, of power, privilege, or dominance. What makes it sex discrimination, as opposed to the actions of 'a philanderer, a terrible person, and a cheapskate,' or a racist for that matter, is not the fact that the conduct is sexual, but that the sexual conduct is being used to enforce or perpetuate gender norms and stereotypes." Id. at 744–45.

5. Professor Franke traces much of the difficulty in the same-sex cases to a confusion about the underpinnings of sexual harassment generally. While *Meritor* was a great step forward, it did not explicitly choose between three competing theories urged by feminist theorists of what made a particular act discrimination on account of sex: "(1) the equality principle: the conduct would not have been undertaken but for the plaintiff's sex; (2) the anti-sex principle: the conduct was discriminatory precisely because it was sexual; and (3) the anti-subordination principle: the conduct subordinated women to men." Id. at 705. How might these different approaches affect the outcome of a same-sex harassment case?

6. One test case is the "equal opportunity harasser," the person who directs offensive conduct and remarks against both men and women. At least under the "equality" approach, such a person is not guilty of sex discrimination under Title VII. Charles R. Calleros, The Meaning of "Sex": Homosexual and Bisexual Harassment under Title VII, 20 Vt. L. Rev. 55, 70-78 (1995). See also Ramona L. Paetzold, Same-Sex Harassment: Can It Be Sex-Related for Purposes of Title VII?, 1 Employee Rts. & Employment Policy J. 25 (1997). But under the "sexual conduct is discriminatory" approach, the result might be different. What about the anti-subordination principle? While this theory would prohibit sexual harassment because of its tendency to subordinate women in the workplace, might such subordination be implicit in any attempt to confine either sex to traditional gender roles?

7. The district court in Johnson v. Tower Air, Inc., 149 F.R.D. 461, 469 (E.D.N.Y. 1993), apparently used the equality model in dismissing a case:

> Clearly, Paladines was not a pleasant person for whom or with whom to work; plaintiff's . . . deposition testimony ma[kes] that fact abundantly clear. However, another fact that is clear is that Paladines was unpleasant to each member of the crew, irrespective of their sex; moreover, his comments to Johnson, although undisputedly offensive, when examined in context appear far more hostile and angry than they do sexual. Behavior that is immature, nasty, or annoying, without more, is not actionable as sexual harassment.

Compare Chiapuzio v. BLT Operating Corp., 826 F. Supp. 1334 (D. Wyo. 1993), where a supervisor subjected both male and female employees to sexually offensive remarks, including boasts regarding his sexual prowess and graphic descriptions of sexual acts he wished to perform with female employees. The court found that the remarks made to male employees were designed to harass men and the remarks made to female employees were designed to harass women. It held for the plaintiffs, concluding that "it is not un-thinkable to argue that each individual who is harassed is being treated badly because of gender." Id. at 1337 (quoting John J. Donohue, Advocacy Versus Analysis in Assessing Employment Discrimination Law, 44 Stan. L. Rev. 1583, 1610-1611 (1992)). Are these cases necessarily inconsistent?

8. How should courts respond when an individual complains about of-fensive remarks made by a supervisor to workers of one gender that would of-fend both men and women? See Fair v. Guiding Eyes for the Blind, 742 F. Supp. 151 (S.D.N.Y. 1990) (no violation). No matter what form the offensive behavior takes, if it is directed only at one gender, isn't that sex discrimina-tion? What about remarks made to one or both genders that, because of their content, are offensive or disparaging only to individuals of one gender? Of course, even if the remarks are found to be sex-based, they must still alter the terms and conditions of a reasonable victim's employment to be actionable.

9. If Oncale's employer can establish that his co-workers harassed him be-cause he is a homosexual, can he nonetheless establish an actionable claim under Title VII? How? In Subsection C.4 of this chapter, we will see that dis-crimination on the basis of sexual preference is not generally actionable un-der Title VII. Some have argued that this means that gays and lesbians can never be protected by Title VII, but that cases like Oncale subject them to the statute's sanctions. Is this problematic? Given the lack of federal protection against discrimination on grounds of sexual orientation, there has been con-siderable debate in the literature about whether recognizing same-sex harass-ment as actionable will alleviate or contribute to the subordination of gays and lesbians in the workplace. See generally Richard F. Storrow, Same-Sex Sexual Harassment Claims After Oncale: Defining the Boundaries of Ac-tionable Conduct, 47 Am. U. L. Rev. 677 (1998).

11. In discussing the requirement that conduct be severe or pervasive to be actionable, the Oncale Court states, "in same-sex (as in all) harassment cases, that inquiry requires careful consideration of the social context in which particular behavior occurs and is experienced by its target." Does this mean that it is not possible to establish sexual harassment when females are hired to work in a previously all-male blue collar workplace where sexually explicit language and pictures have long been commonplace?

12. If Oncale requires a reconsideration of what "because of sex" means, perhaps the following extract from Vicki Schultz, Reconceptualizing Sex-ual Harassment 107 Yale L.J. 1683, 1686-1687, 1689 (1998), will help with that task:

> That feminists (and sympathetic lawyers) have inspired a body of popular and le-gal opinion condemning harassment in such a brief period of time is a remark-able achievement. Yet the achievement has been limited because we have not conceptualized the problem in sufficiently broad terms. The prevailing para-digm for understanding sex-based harassment places sexuality — more specifi-cally, male-female sexual advances — at the center of the problem. Within that

paradigm, a male supervisor's sexual advances on a less powerful, female subordinate represent the quintessential form of harassment.

Although this sexual desire-dominance paradigm represented progress when it was first articulated as the foundation for quid pro quo sexual harassment, using the paradigm to conceptualize hostile work environment harassment has served to exclude from legal understanding many of the most common and debilitating forms of harassment faced by women (and many men) at work each day. The prevailing paradigm privileges conduct thought to be motivated by sexual designs — such as sexual advances — as the core sex- or gender-based harassment. Yet much of the gender-based hostility and abuse that women (and some men) endure at work is neither driven by the desire for sexual relations nor even sexual in content. . . .

This Article challenges the sexual desire-dominance paradigm. A comprehensive examination of Title VII hostile work environment harassment cases demonstrates the paradigm's inadequacy. Despite the best intentions of its creators, the paradigm has compromised the law's protection. Principal among its drawbacks, the paradigm is underinclusive: It omits — and even obscures — many of the most prevalent forms of harassment that make workplaces hostile and alienating to workers based on their gender. Much of what is harmful to women in the workplace is difficult to construe as sexual in design. Similarly, many men are harmed at work by gender-based harassment that fits only uneasily within the parameters of a sexualized paradigm. The prevailing paradigm, however, may also be overinclusive. By emphasizing the protection of women's sexual selves and sensibilities over and above their empowerment as workers, the paradigm permits — or even encourages — companies to construe the law to prohibit some forms of sexual expression that do not promote gender hierarchy at work. The focus of harassment law should not be on sexuality as such. The focus should be on conduct that consigns people to gendered work roles that do not further their own aspirations or advantage.

Page 651.   Add new Note 3A:

3A. After *Harris*, the Ninth Circuit modified its standard for evaluating sexual harassment in an attempt to reconcile the *Ellison* standard with the standard applied in *Harris*:

> [w]hether the workplace is objectively hostile must be determined from the perspective of a reasonable person with the same fundamental characteristics.

Fuller v. City of Oakland, 47 F.3d 1522, 1527 (9th Cir. 1995). See also Crowe v. Wiltel Communications Sys., 103 F.3d 897 (9th Cir. 1996).

Page 661.   Add at end of the carryover paragraph:

In two recent decisions, both the Tenth and Eleventh Circuits declined to find sexual harassment liability based on decisions by supervisors favoring employees with whom they had sexual relationships. See Womack v. Runyon, 147 F.3d 1298 (11th Cir. 1998) (preferential treatment based on consensual relationship between supervisor and employee does not constitute a cognizable sex discrimination claim under Title VII); Taken v. Oklahoma Corp. Commn., 125 F.3d 1366 (10th Cir. 1997) (promotion of girlfriend over two other female candidates does not violate Title VII).

Page 665–671. *Delete notes following* **Meritor;** *insert the following principal case and notes:*

BURLINGTON INDUSTRIES, INC. V. ELLERTH
524 U.S. 742 (1998)

Justice KENNEDY delivered the opinion of the Court.

We decide whether, under Title VII of the Civil Rights Act of 1964 an employee who refuses the unwelcome and threatening sexual advances of a supervisor, yet suffers no adverse, tangible job consequences, can recover against the employer without showing the employer is negligent or otherwise at fault for the supervisor's actions.

I

Summary judgment was granted for the employer, so we must take the facts alleged by the employee to be true. The employer is Burlington Industries, the petitioner. The employee is Kimberly Ellerth, the respondent. From March 1993 until May 1994, Ellerth worked as a salesperson in one of Burlington's divisions in Chicago, Illinois. During her employment, she alleges, she was subjected to constant sexual harassment by her supervisor, one Ted Slowik.

In the hierarchy of Burlington's management structure, Slowik was a mid-level manager. Burlington has eight divisions, employing more than 22,000 people in some 50 plants around the United States. Slowik was a vice president in one of five business units within one of the divisions. He had authority to make hiring and promotion decisions subject to the approval of his supervisor, who signed the paperwork. According to Slowik's supervisor, his position was "not considered an upper-level management position," and he was "not amongst the decision-making or policy-making hierarchy." Slowik was not Ellerth's immediate supervisor.

Ellerth worked in a two-person office in Chicago, and she answered to her office colleague, who in turn answered to Slowik in New York.

Against a background of repeated boorish and offensive remarks and gestures which Slowik allegedly made, Ellerth places particular emphasis on three alleged incidents where Slowik's comments could be construed as threats to deny her tangible job benefits. In the summer of 1993, while on a business trip, Slowik invited Ellerth to the hotel lounge, an invitation Ellerth felt compelled to accept because Slowik was her boss. When Ellerth gave no encouragement to remarks Slowik made about her breasts, he told her to "loosen up" and warned, "you know, Kim, I could make your life very hard or very easy at Burlington."

In March 1994, when Ellerth was being considered for a promotion, Slowik expressed reservations during the promotion interview because she was not "loose enough." The comment was followed by his reaching over and rubbing her knee. Ellerth did receive the promotion; but when Slowik called to announce it, he told Ellerth, "you're gonna be out there with men who work in factories, and they certainly like women with pretty butts/legs."

In May 1994, Ellerth called Slowik, asking permission to insert a customer's logo into a fabric sample. Slowik responded, "I don't have time for you right now, Kim — unless you want to tell me what you're wearing." Ellerth told Slowik she had to go and ended the call. A day or two later, Ellerth called Slowik to ask permission again. This time he denied her request, but added something along the lines of, "are you wearing shorter skirts yet, Kim, because it would make your job a whole heck of a lot easier."

A short time later, Ellerth's immediate supervisor cautioned her about returning telephone calls to customers in a prompt fashion. In response, Ellerth quit. She faxed a letter giving reasons unrelated to the alleged sexual harassment we have described. About three weeks later, however, she sent a letter explaining she quit because of Slowik's behavior.

During her tenure at Burlington, Ellerth did not inform anyone in authority about Slowik's conduct, despite knowing Burlington had a policy against sexual harassment. In fact, she chose not to inform her immediate supervisor (not Slowik) because "'it would be his duty as my supervisor to report any incidents of sexual harassment.'" On one occasion, she told Slowik a comment he made was inappropriate.

. . . The District Court granted summary judgment to Burlington. The Court found Slowik's behavior, as described by Ellerth, severe and pervasive enough to create a hostile work environment, but found Burlington neither knew nor should have known about the conduct. . . .

The Court of Appeals en banc reversed in a decision which produced eight separate opinions and no consensus for a controlling rationale. The judges were able to agree on the problem they confronted: Vicarious liability, not failure to comply with a duty of care, was the essence of Ellerth's case against Burlington on appeal. The judges seemed to agree Ellerth could recover if Slowik's unfulfilled threats to deny her tangible job benefits was sufficient to impose vicarious liability on Burlington. With the exception of Judges Coffey and Easterbrook, the judges also agreed Ellerth's claim could be categorized as one of quid pro quo harassment, even though she had received the promotion and had suffered no other tangible retaliation.

The consensus disintegrated on the standard for an employer's liability for such a claim. . . . The disagreement revealed in the careful opinions of the judges of the Court of Appeals reflects the fact that Congress has left it to the courts to determine controlling agency law principles in a new and difficult area of federal law. We granted certiorari to assist in defining the relevant standards of employer liability.

II

At the outset, we assume an important proposition yet to be established before a trier of fact. It is a premise assumed as well, in explicit or implicit terms, in the various opinions by the judges of the Court of Appeals. The premise is: a trier of fact could find in Slowik's remarks numerous threats to retaliate against Ellerth if she denied some sexual liberties. The threats, however, were not carried out or fulfilled. Cases based on threats which are carried out are referred to often as quid pro quo cases, as distinct from bothersome attentions or sexual remarks that are sufficiently severe or pervasive to create a hostile work environment. The terms quid pro quo and hostile work environment are helpful, perhaps, in making a rough demarcation between cases in which threats are carried out and those where they are not or are absent altogether, but beyond this are of limited utility.

Section 703(a) of Title VII forbids "an employer"—

(1) to fail or refuse to hire or to discharge any individual, or otherwise to discriminate against any individual with respect to his compensation, terms, conditions or privileges of employment, because of such individual's . . . sex.

"Quid pro quo" and "hostile work environment" do not appear in the statutory text. The terms appeared first in the academic literature, found their way into decisions of the Courts of Appeals, and were mentioned in this Court's decision in *Meritor.*

In *Meritor,* the terms served a specific and limited purpose. There we considered whether the conduct in question constituted discrimination in the terms or conditions of employment in violation of Title VII. We assumed, and with adequate reason, that if an employer demanded sexual favors from an employee in return for a job benefit, discrimination with respect to terms or conditions of employment was explicit. Less obvious was whether an employer's sexually demeaning behavior altered terms or conditions of employment in violation of Title VII. We distinguished between quid pro quo claims and hostile environment claims, and said both were cognizable under Title VII, though the latter requires harassment that is severe or pervasive. The principal significance of the distinction is to instruct that Title VII is violated by either explicit or constructive alterations in the terms or conditions of employment and to explain the latter must be severe or pervasive. The distinction was not discussed for its bearing upon an employer's liability for an employee's discrimination. On this question *Meritor* held, with no further specifics, that agency principles controlled.

Nevertheless, as use of the terms grew in the wake of *Meritor,* they acquired their own significance. The standard of employer responsibility turned on which type of harassment occurred. If the plaintiff established a quid pro quo claim, the Courts of Appeals held, the employer was subject to vicarious liability. The rule encouraged Title VII plaintiffs to state their claims as quid pro quo claims, which in turn put expansive pressure on the definition. The equivalence of the quid pro quo label and vicarious liability is illustrated by this case. The question presented on certiorari is whether Ellerth can state a claim of quid pro quo harassment, but the issue of real concern to the parties is whether Burlington has vicarious liability for Slowik's alleged misconduct, rather than liability limited to its own negligence. . . .

We do not suggest the terms quid pro quo and hostile work environment are irrelevant to Title VII litigation. To the extent they illustrate the distinction between cases involving a threat which is carried out and offensive conduct in general, the terms are relevant when there is a threshold question whether a plaintiff can prove discrimination in violation of Title VII. When a plaintiff proves that a tangible employment action resulted from a refusal to submit to a supervisor's sexual demands, he or she establishes that the employment decision itself constitutes a change in the terms and conditions of employment that is actionable under Title VII. For any sexual harassment preceding the employment decision to be actionable, however, the conduct must be severe or pervasive. Because Ellerth's claim involves only unfulfilled threats, it should be categorized as a hostile work environment claim which requires a showing of severe or pervasive conduct. For purposes of this case, we accept the District Court's finding that the alleged conduct was severe or pervasive. The case before us involves numerous alleged threats, and we express no opinion as to whether a single unfulfilled threat is sufficient to constitute discrimination in the terms or conditions of employment.

When we assume discrimination can be proved, however, the factors we discuss below, and not the categories quid pro quo and hostile work environment, will be controlling on the issue of vicarious liability. That is the question we must resolve.

III

We must decide, then, whether an employer has vicarious liability when a supervisor creates a hostile work environment by making explicit threats to alter a subordinate's terms or conditions of employment, based on sex, but does not fulfill the threat. We turn to principles of agency law, for the term "employer" is defined under Title VII to include "agents." In express terms, Congress has directed federal courts to interpret Title VII based on agency principles. Given such an explicit instruction, we conclude a uniform and predictable standard must be established as a matter of federal law. We rely "on the general common law of agency, rather than on the law of any partic-

C. Gender Discrimination

ular State, to give meaning to these terms." Community for Creative Non-Violence v. Reid, 490 U.S. 730, 740 (1989). The resulting federal rule, based on a body of case law developed over time, is statutory interpretation pursuant to congressional direction. This is not federal common law in "the strictest sense, i.e., a rule of decision that amounts, not simply to an interpretation of a federal statute . . . , but, rather, to the judicial 'creation' of a special federal rule of decision." Atherton v. FDIC, 519 U.S. 213, 218 (1997). . . .

As *Meritor* acknowledged, the Restatement (Second) of Agency (1957) (hereinafter Restatement), is a useful beginning point for a discussion of general agency principles. Since our decision in *Meritor*, federal courts have explored agency principles, and we find useful instruction in their decisions, noting that "common-law principles may not be transferable in all their particulars to Title VII." The EEOC has issued Guidelines governing sexual harassment claims under Title VII, but they provide little guidance on the issue of employer liability for supervisor harassment. See 29 CFR § 1604.11(c) (1997) (vicarious liability for supervisor harassment turns on "the particular employment relationship and the job functions performed by the individual").

A

Section 219(1) of the Restatement sets out a central principle of agency law:

> A master is subject to liability for the torts of his servants committed while acting in the scope of their employment.

An employer may be liable for both negligent and intentional torts committed by an employee within the scope of his or her employment. Sexual harassment under Title VII presupposes intentional conduct. While early decisions absolved employers of liability for the intentional torts of their employees, the law now imposes liability where the employee's "purpose, however misguided, is wholly or in part to further the master's business." W. Keeton, D. Dobbs, R. Keeton, & D. Owen, Prosser and Keeton on Law of Torts § 70, p. 505 (5th ed. 1984) (hereinafter Prosser and Keeton on Torts). In applying scope of employment principles to intentional torts, however, it is accepted that "it is less likely that a willful tort will properly be held to be in the course of employment and that the liability of the master for such torts will naturally be more limited." F. Mechem, Outlines of the Law of Agency § 394, p. 266 (P. Mechem 4th ed. 1952). The Restatement defines conduct, including an intentional tort, to be within the scope of employment when "actuated, at least in part, by a purpose to serve the [employer]," even if it is forbidden by the employer. Restatement §§ 228(1)(c), 230.

As Courts of Appeals have recognized, a supervisor acting out of gender-based animus or a desire to fulfill sexual urges may not be actuated by a purpose to serve the employer. The harassing supervisor often acts for personal motives, motives unrelated and even antithetical to the objectives of the employer. There are instances, of course, where a supervisor engages in unlawful discrimination with the purpose, mistaken or otherwise, to serve the employer.

The general rule is that sexual harassment by a supervisor is not conduct within the scope of employment.

B

Scope of employment does not define the only basis for employer liability under agency principles. In limited circumstances, agency principles impose liability on employers even where employees commit torts outside the scope of employment. The principles are set forth in the much-cited § 219(2) of the Restatement:

> (2) A master is not subject to liability for the torts of his servants acting outside the scope of their employment, unless:
>
> (a) the master intended the conduct or the consequences, or
> (b) the master was negligent or reckless, or
> (c) the conduct violated a non-delegable duty of the master, or
> (d) the servant purported to act or to speak on behalf of the principal and there was reliance upon apparent authority, or he was aided in accomplishing the tort by the existence of the agency relation.

Subsection (a) addresses direct liability, where the employer acts with tortious intent, and indirect liability, where the agent's high rank in the company makes him or her the employer's alter ego. None of the parties contend Slowik's rank imputes liability under this principle. There is no contention, furthermore, that a non-delegable duty is involved. See § 219(2)(c). So, for our purposes here, subsections (a) and (c) can be put aside.

Subsections (b) and (d) are possible grounds for imposing employer liability on account of a supervisor's acts and must be considered. Under subsection (b), an employer is liable when the tort is attributable to the employer's own negligence. Thus, although a supervisor's sexual harassment is outside the scope of employment because the conduct was for personal motives, an employer can be liable, nonetheless, where its own negligence is a cause of the harassment. An employer is negligent with respect to sexual harassment if it knew or should have known about the conduct and failed to stop it. Negligence sets a minimum standard for employer liability under Title VII; but Ellerth seeks to invoke the more stringent standard of vicarious liability.

Subsection 219(2)(d) concerns vicarious liability for intentional torts committed by an employee when the employee uses apparent authority (the apparent authority standard), or when the employee "was aided in accomplishing the tort by the existence of the agency relation" (the aided in the agency relation standard). As other federal decisions have done in discussing vicarious liability for supervisor harassment, we begin with § 219(2)(d).

C. Gender Discrimination

C

As a general rule, apparent authority is relevant where the agent purports to exercise a power which he or she does not have, as distinct from where the agent threatens to misuse actual power. In the usual case, a supervisor's harassment involves misuse of actual power, not the false impression of its existence. Apparent authority analysis therefore is inappropriate in this context. If, in the unusual case, it is alleged there is a false impression that the actor was a supervisor, when he in fact was not, the victim's mistaken conclusion must be a reasonable one. When a party seeks to impose vicarious liability based on an agent's misuse of delegated authority, the Restatement's aided in the agency relation rule, rather than the apparent authority rule, appears to be the appropriate form of analysis.

D

We turn to the aided in the agency relation standard. In a sense, most workplace tortfeasors are aided in accomplishing their tortious objective by the existence of the agency relation: Proximity and regular contact may afford a captive pool of potential victims. Were this to satisfy the aided in the agency relation standard, an employer would be subject to vicarious liability not only for all supervisor harassment, but also for all co-worker harassment, a result enforced by neither the EEOC nor any court of appeals to have considered the issue. The aided in the agency relation standard, therefore, requires the existence of something more than the employment relation itself.

At the outset, we can identify a class of cases where, beyond question, more than the mere existence of the employment relation aids in commission of the harassment: when a supervisor takes a tangible employment action against the subordinate. Every Federal Court of Appeals to have considered the question has found vicarious liability when a discriminatory act results in a tangible employment action. In *Meritor*, we acknowledged this consensus ("The courts have consistently held employers liable for the discriminatory discharges of employees by supervisory personnel, whether or not the employer knew, or should have known, or approved of the supervisor's actions"). Although few courts have elaborated how agency principles support this rule, we think it reflects a correct application of the aided in the agency relation standard.

In the context of this case, a tangible employment action would have taken the form of a denial of a raise or a promotion. The concept of a tangible employment action appears in numerous cases in the Courts of Appeals discussing claims involving race, age, and national origin discrimination, as well as sex discrimination. Without endorsing the specific results of those decisions, we think it prudent to import the concept of a tangible employment action for resolution of the vicarious liability issue we consider here. A tangible employment action constitutes a significant change in employment status, such as hiring, firing, failing to promote, reassignment with significantly different responsibilities, or a decision causing a significant change in benefits. Compare Crady v. Liberty Nat'l Bank & Trust Co. of Ind., 993 F.2d 132, 136 (7th Cir. 1993) ("A materially adverse change might be indicated by a termination of employment, a demotion evidenced by a decrease in wage or salary, a less distinguished title, a material loss of benefits, significantly diminished material responsibilities, or other indices that might be unique to a particular situation"), with Flaherty v. Gas Research Institute, 31 F.3d 451, 456 (7th Cir. 1994) (a "bruised ego" is not enough); Kocsis v. Multi-Care Management, Inc., 97 F.3d 876, 887 (6th Cir. 1996) (demotion without change in pay, benefits, duties, or prestige insufficient) and Harlston v. McDonnell Douglas Corp., 37 F.3d 379, 382 (8th Cir. 1994) (reassignment to more inconvenient job insufficient).

When a supervisor makes a tangible employment decision, there is assurance the injury could not have been inflicted absent the agency relation. A tangible employment action in most cases inflicts direct economic harm. As a general proposition, only a supervisor, or other person acting with the authority of the company, can cause this sort of injury. A co-worker can break a co-worker's arm as easily as a supervisor, and anyone who has regular contact with an employee can inflict psychological injuries by his or her offensive conduct. But one co-worker (absent some elaborate scheme) cannot dock another's pay, nor can one co-worker demote another. Tangible employment actions fall within the special province of the supervisor. The supervisor has been empowered by the company as a distinct class of agent to make economic decisions affecting other employees under his or her control.

Tangible employment actions are the means by which the supervisor brings the official power of the enterprise to bear on subordinates. A tangible employment decision requires an official act of the enterprise, a company act. The decision in most cases is documented in official company records, and may be subject to review by higher level supervisors. The supervisor often must obtain the imprimatur of the enterprise and use its internal processes.

For these reasons, a tangible employment action taken by the supervisor becomes for Title VII purposes the act of the employer. Whatever the exact contours of the aided in the agency relation standard, its requirements will always be met when a supervisor takes a tangible employment action against a subordinate. In that instance, it would be implausible to interpret agency principles to allow an employer to escape liability, as *Meritor* itself appeared to acknowledge.

Whether the agency relation aids in commission of supervisor harassment which does not culminate in a tangible employment action is less obvious. Application of the standard is made difficult by its malleable terminology, which can be read to either expand or limit liability in the context of supervisor harassment. On the one hand, a supervisor's power and authority invests his or her harassing conduct with a particular threatening character, and in this sense, a supervisor always is aided by the agency relation. See *Meritor.* (Marshall, J., concurring in judgment) ("It is precisely because the supervisor is understood to be clothed with the employer's authority that he is able to impose unwelcome sexual conduct on subordinates"). On the other hand, there are acts of harassment a supervisor might commit which might be the same acts a co-employee would commit, and there may be some circumstances where the supervisor's status makes little difference.

It is this tension which, we think, has caused so much confusion among the Courts of Appeals which have sought to apply the aided in the agency relation standard to Title VII cases. The aided in the agency relation standard, however, is a developing feature of agency law, and we hesitate to render a definitive explanation of our understanding of the standard in an area where other important considerations must affect our judgment. In particular, we are bound by our holding in *Meritor* that agency principles constrain the imposition of vicarious liability in cases of supervisory harassment. See *Meritor* ("Congress' decision to define 'employer' to include any 'agent' of an employer, 42 U.S.C. § 2000e(b), surely evinces an intent to place some limits on the acts of employees for which employers under Title VII are to be held responsible"). Congress has not altered *Meritor's* rule even though it has made significant amendments to Title VII in the interim. Although *Meritor* suggested the limitation on employer liability stemmed from agency principles, the Court acknowledged other considerations might be relevant as well. For example, Title VII is designed to encourage the creation of antiharassment policies and effective grievance mechanisms. Were employer liability to depend in part on an employer's effort to create such procedures, it would effect Congress' intention to promote conciliation rather than litigation in the Title VII context and the EEOC's policy of encouraging the development of grievance procedures. See 29 CFR § 1604.11(f) (1997); EEOC Policy Guidance on Sexual Harassment, 8 BNA FEP Manual 405:6699 (Mar. 19, 1990). To the extent limiting employer liability could encourage employees to report harassing conduct before it becomes severe or pervasive, it would also serve Title VII's deterrent purpose. As we have observed, Title VII borrows from tort law the avoidable consequences doctrine, and the considerations which animate that doctrine would also support the limitation of employer liability in certain circumstances.

In order to accommodate the agency principles of vicarious liability for harm caused by misuse of supervisory authority, as well as Title VII's equally basic policies of encouraging forethought by employers and saving action by objecting employees, we adopt the following holding in this case and in Faragher v. Boca Raton, also decided today. An employer is subject to vicarious liability to a victimized employee for an actionable hostile environment created by a supervisor with immediate (or successively higher) authority over the employee. When no tangible employment action is taken, a defending employer may raise an affirmative defense to liability or damages, subject to proof by a preponderance of the evidence. The defense comprises two necessary elements: (a) that the employer exercised reasonable care to prevent and correct promptly any sexually harassing behavior, and (b) that the plaintiff employee unreasonably failed to take advantage of any preventive or corrective opportunities provided by the employer or to avoid harm otherwise. While proof that an employer had promulgated an anti-harassment policy with complaint procedure is not necessary in every instance as a matter of law, the need for a stated policy suitable to the employment circumstances may appropriately be addressed in any case when litigating the first element of the defense. And while proof that an employee failed to fulfill the corresponding obligation of reasonable care to avoid harm is not limited to showing any unreasonable failure to use any complaint procedure provided by the employer, a demonstration of such failure will normally suffice to satisfy the employer's burden under the second element of the defense. No affirmative defense is available, however, when the supervisor's harassment culminates in a tangible employment action, such as discharge, demotion, or undesirable reassignment.

IV

Relying on existing case law which held out the promise of vicarious liability for all quid pro quo claims, Ellerth focused all her attention in the Court of Appeals on proving her claim fit within that category. Given our explanation that the labels quid pro quo and hostile work environment are not controlling for purposes of establishing employer liability, Ellerth should have an adequate opportunity to prove she has a claim for which Burlington is liable.

Although Ellerth has not alleged she suffered a tangible employment action at the hands of Slowik, which would deprive Burlington of the availability of the affirmative defense, this is not dispositive. In light of our decision, Burlington is still subject to vicarious liability for Slowik's activity, but Burlington should have an opportunity to assert and prove the affirmative defense to liability. . . .

NOTES

1. *Meritor* did not fully resolve one of the major issues in sexual harassment cases — under what circumstances is the *employer* liable for harassment in the workplace? Nevertheless, the court clearly did not impose liability automatically. Resolving this issue is particularly important because, although Title VII defines "employer" to include "any agent" of an employer, courts have not always been willing to hold individual employees personally liable for their discriminatory conduct. See Chapter 11. If employers are not liable

for their supervisor's conduct, it is possible that neither the individual harasser nor the employer will be liable in some circumstances. In *Ellerth*, the court sought to clarify employers' liability for supervisors' actions. In *Faragher v. City of Boca Raton*, 141 L. Ed. 2d 662 (1998), a companion case to *Ellerth*, the Court also considered the liability of an employer for the harassing actions of its supervisor. In *Faragher*, the Court adopted the same holding as in *Ellerth* based on the following analysis:

> We . . . agree with Faragher that in implementing Title VII it makes sense to hold an employer vicariously liable for some tortious conduct of a supervisor made possible by abuse of his supervisory authority, and that the aided-by-agency-relation principle embodied in § 219(2)(d) of the Restatement provides an appropriate starting point for determining liability for the kind of harassment presented here. Several courts, indeed, have noted what Faragher has argued, that there is a sense in which a harassing supervisor is always assisted in his misconduct by the supervisory relationship. See, e.g., Rodgers v. Western-Southern Life Ins. Co., 12 F.3d 668, 675 (7th Cir. 1993); Taylor v. Metzger, 706 A.2d 685, 692 (1998) (emphasizing that a supervisor's conduct may have a greater impact than that of colleagues at the same level). The agency relationship affords contact with an employee subjected to a supervisor's sexual harassment, and the victim may well be reluctant to accept the risks of blowing the whistle on a superior. When a person with supervisory authority discriminates in the terms and conditions of subordinates' employment, his actions necessarily draw upon his superior position over the people who report to him, or those under them, whereas an employee generally cannot check a supervisor's abusive conduct the same way that she might deal with abuse from a co-worker. When a fellow employee harasses, the victim can walk away or tell the offender where to go, but it may be difficult to offer such responses to a supervisor, whose "power to supervise — [which may be] to hire and fire, and to set work schedules and pay rates — does not disappear . . . when he chooses to harass through insults and offensive gestures rather than directly with threats of firing or promises of promotion." Estrich, Sex at Work, 43 Stan. L. Rev. 813, 854 (1991). Recognition of employer liability when discriminatory misuse of supervisory authority alters the terms and conditions of a victim's employment is underscored by the fact that the employer has a greater opportunity to guard against misconduct by supervisors than by common workers; employers have greater opportunity and incentive to screen them, train them, and monitor their performance.
>
> In sum, there are good reasons for vicarious liability for misuse of supervisory authority. That rationale must, however, satisfy one more condition. We are not entitled to recognize this theory under Title VII unless we can square it with *Meritor's* holding that an employer is not "automatically" liable for harassment by a supervisor who creates the requisite degree of discrimination, and there is obviously some tension between that holding and the position that a supervisor's misconduct aided by supervisory authority subjects the employer to liability vicariously; if the "aid" may be the unspoken suggestion of retaliation by misuse of supervisory authority, the risk of automatic liability is high. To counter it, we think there are two basic alternatives, one being to require proof

of some affirmative invocation of that authority by the harassing supervisor, the other to recognize an affirmative defense to liability in some circumstances, even when a supervisor has created the actionable environment.

There is certainly some authority for requiring active or affirmative, as distinct from passive or implicit, misuse of supervisory authority before liability may be imputed. That is the way some courts have viewed the familiar cases holding the employer liable for discriminatory employment action with tangible consequences, like firing and demotion. And we have already noted some examples of liability provided by the Restatement itself, which suggests that an affirmative misuse of power might be required.

But neat examples illustrating the line between the affirmative and merely implicit uses of power are not easy to come by in considering management behavior. Supervisors do not make speeches threatening sanctions whenever they make requests in the legitimate exercise of managerial authority, and yet every subordinate employee knows the sanctions exist; this is the reason that courts have consistently held that acts of supervisors have greater power to alter the environment than acts of co-employees generally. How far from the course of ostensible supervisory behavior would a company officer have to step before his orders would not reasonably be seen as actively using authority? Judgment calls would often be close, the results would often seem disparate even if not demonstrably contradictory, and the temptation to litigate would be hard to resist. We think plaintiffs and defendants alike would be poorly served by an active-use rule.

The other basic alternative to automatic liability would avoid this particular temptation to litigate, but allow an employer to show as an affirmative defense to liability that the employer had exercised reasonable care to avoid harassment and to eliminate it when it might occur, and that the complaining employee had failed to act with like reasonable care to take advantage of the employer's safeguards and otherwise to prevent harm that could have been avoided. This composite defense would, we think, implement the statute sensibly, for reasons that are not hard to fathom.

Although Title VII seeks "to make persons whole for injuries suffered on account of unlawful employment discrimination," Albemarle Paper Co. v. Moody, its "primary objective," like that of any statute meant to influence primary conduct, is not to provide redress but to avoid harm. As long ago as 1980, the Equal Employment Opportunity Commission (EEOC), charged with the enforcement of Title VII, adopted regulations advising employers to "take all steps necessary to prevent sexual harassment from occurring, such as . . . informing employees of their right to raise and how to raise the issue of harassment." 29 CFR § 1604.11(f) (1997), and in 1990 the Commission issued a policy statement enjoining employers to establish a complaint procedure "designed to encourage victims of harassment to come forward [without requiring] a victim to complain first to the offending supervisor." EEOC Policy Guidance on Sexual Harassment, 8 FEP Manual 405:6699 (Mar. 19, 1990) (internal quotation marks omitted). It would therefore implement clear statutory policy and complement the Government's Title VII enforcement efforts to recognize the employer's affirmative obligation to prevent violations and give credit here to employers who make reasonable efforts to discharge their duty. Indeed, a theory of vicarious liability for misuse of supervisory power would be at odds with the statutory policy if it failed to provide employers with some such incentive.

The requirement to show that the employee has failed in a coordinate duty to avoid or mitigate harm reflects an equally obvious policy imported from the general theory of damages, that a victim has a duty "to use such means as are reasonable under the circumstances to avoid or minimize the damages" that result from violations of the statute. Ford Motor Co. v. EEOC, 458 U.S. 219, 231, n. 15 (1982) (quoting C. McCormick, Law of Damages 127 (1935)) (internal quotation marks omitted). An employer may, for example, have provided a proven, effective mechanism for reporting and resolving complaints of sexual harassment, available to the employee without undue risk or expense. If the plaintiff unreasonably failed to avail herself of the employer's preventive or remedial apparatus, she should not recover damages that could have been avoided if she had done so. If the victim could have avoided harm, no liability should be found against the employer who had taken reasonable care, and if damages could reasonably have been mitigated no award against a liable employer should reward a plaintiff for what her own efforts could have avoided.

In order to accommodate the principle of vicarious liability for harm caused by misuse of supervisory authority, as well as Title VII's equally basic policies of encouraging forethought by employers and saving action by objecting employees, we adopt the following holding in this case and in Burlington Industries, Inc. v. Ellerth, also decided today.

Id. at 685-86. Did the Court in *Ellerth* and *Faragher* create a rule of liability that is fair to plaintiffs? Is this rule fair to defendants?

2. When *Meritor* was decided, the only remedy for hostile environment harassment was injunctive relief. It mattered little, therefore, *when* an employer became responsible. With compensatory damages available under the 1991 amendments, the question is more pointed because harassment may go on for a substantial period of time before an agent of the employer other than the harasser becomes aware of it. The Court, in *Ellerth* and in footnote 4 of *Faragher,* emphasized the importance of following *Meritor's* holding relieving employers of automatic liability for supervisor harassment on the ground that Congress enacted the 1991 amendments, with their imposition of compensatory and emotional distress damages, with *Meritor's* limitation on liability in mind.

3. Prior to *Ellerth,* courts held that, if the harasser is himself in a high enough position in the employer's hierarchy, the actions and knowledge of the harasser are imputed to the employer, what *Ellerth* referred to as "alter ego" liability. See, e.g., Lankford v. City of Hobart, 27 F.3d 477 (10th Cir. 1994); Kotcher v. Rosa & Sullivan Appliance Ctr., Inc., 957 F.2d 59 (2d Cir. 1992). In *Faragher,* the Court made the following remarks with respect to imputed liability:

[It was not] exceptional that standards for binding the employer were not in issue in *Harris.* In that case of discrimination by hostile environment, the individual charged with creating the abusive atmosphere was the president of the corporate employer, who was indisputably within that class of an employer organization's officials who may be treated as the organization's proxy. Burns v. McGregor Electronic Industries, Inc., 955 F.2d 559, 564 (8th Cir. 1992) (employer-company liable where harassment was perpetrated by its owner); see Torres v. Pisano, 116 F.3d 625, 634-635, and n. 11 (2d Cir.) (noting that a supervisor may hold a sufficiently high position "in the management hierarchy of the company for his actions to be imputed automatically to the employer"), cert. denied, 522 U.S.__(1997).

141 L. Ed.2d at 677. Is the defense created in *Ellerth* and *Faragher* available in cases in which the harasser's actions are imputed to the employer under the "alter ego" or "proxy" approach?

4. After *Ellerth*, is it possible to argue that in some cases sexual harassment by a supervisor is "within the scope of employment" of the supervisor? Suppose a supervisor requires female employees to wear revealing attire that generates severe and pervasive responses by customers? See EEOC v. Sage Realty Co., 507 F. Supp. 599 (S.D.N.Y. 1981) If employer liability can be based on harassment being "within the scope of employment" of a supervisor, is the defense created in *Ellerth* available in such cases or is it available only when "agency" is based on the "aided in the agency relation" approach and no "tangible employment actions" are involved?

5. *Ellerth* distinguishes between quid pro quo and hostile environment cases on the basis of the proof required. Plaintiffs alleging quid pro quo harassment are not required to prove that the harassment was severe or pervasive. Does the plaintiff gain any other advantages by characterizing his or her claim as a quid pro quo claim?

6. Prior to *Ellerth*, the courts generally agreed that the employer is liable for the harassing conduct of co-workers only if the employer knew or should have known of the harassment and failed to take adequate corrective action. Did *Ellerth* change this rule? Who bears the burden of establishing that the employer knew or should have known about co-worker harassment?

7. Even in cases of co-worker harassment, the issue of who the "employer" is and when the employer "knows" about the harassment can arise. In Juarez v. Ameritech Mobile Communications, Inc., 957 F.2d 317 (7th Cir. 1992), plaintiff filed a formal complaint after nearly two months of harassment by a co-worker; AMCI immediately investigated the complaint and disciplined the harasser by suspending him for one week without pay. Juarez experienced no further harassment but nevertheless sued, claiming that her employer was liable for the harassment that occurred prior to her formal complaint because AMCI had "knowledge of prior sexual harassment by [the co-worker] on which it failed to act." Id. at 320. The basis for this claim was evidence that an accounts payable supervisor told Juarez that the harasser was a "'pervert' who had 'bothered' other employees in the past." Id. at 319. The court held that the supervisor's knowledge could not be imputed to AMCI:

> Knowledge of an agent is imputed to her corporate principal only if the agent receives the knowledge while acting within the scope of her authority *and* the knowledge concerns a matter within the scope of that authority. "Further, for knowledge to be imputed, the agent must have not just a duty in relation to the subject matter, but a duty to speak to his principal about the specific item of knowledge."

Id. at 321. Applying this standard, the court concluded that the supervisor's knowledge could not be imputed because, although technically a manager, she supervised only one employee, was not a part of the Human Resources Department, and did not have any supervisory authority over the harasser. Finally, AMCI's sexual harassment policy did not impose any duty on supervisors to report suspected cases of sexual harassment.

8. Does *Ellerth* indicate how to resolve the issue of who the "employer" is for purposes of receiving complaints about harassment by co-workers? Is it sufficient that the worker inform his or her supervisor of harassment by a co-worker if the employer's harassment policy assigns the task of taking complaints to the Human Resources Department? After *Ellerth*, who bears the burden of establishing that an appropriate agent of the employer knew or should have known of co-worker harassment? See Coates v. Sundor Brands, 160 F.3d 688 (11th Cir. 1998) (agency relationship makes employer liable not only for harassment by a supervisor, but also for a supervisors failure to act to abate harassment by an employee's coworkers); Williamson v. City of Houston, 148 F.3d 462 (5th Cir. 1998) (employer's policy directing employees to report harassment to supervisors establishes that supervisor's knowledge of harassment is imputed to the employer).

9. Both *Ellerth* and *Juarez* clearly favor internal resolution of harassment complaints by encouraging victims of harassment to report the problem to individuals with the duty and authority to respond. But do these cases go too far? What if it is common knowledge throughout a department that an employee is being sexually harassed by a co-worker and only the harasser's supervisor is unaware? What if the whole department is aware that a supervisor is harassing an employee, but the Human Resources officer who handles harassment complaints is unaware? Under *Ellerth* and *Juarez*, is the employer considered to have no knowledge and no obligation to take corrective action? In *Faragher*, the Court commented on situations in which knowledge of harassing behavior is widespread in a company:

> There have . . . been myriad cases in which District Courts and Courts of Appeals have held employers liable on account of actual knowledge by the employer, or high-echelon officials of an employer organization, of sufficiently harassing action by subordinates, which the employer or its informed officers have done nothing to stop. See, e.g., Katz v. Dole, 709 F.2d 251, 256 (4th Cir. 1983) (upholding employer liability because the "employer's supervisory personnel manifested unmistakable acquiescence in or approval of the harass-

ment"); EEOC v. Hacienda Hotel, 881 F.2d 1504, 1516 (9th Cir. 1989) (employer liable where hotel manager did not respond to complaints about supervisors' harassment); Hall v. Gus Constr. Co., 842 F.2d 1010, 1016 (8th Cir. 1988) (holding employer liable for harassment by co-workers because supervisor knew of the harassment but did nothing). In such instances, the combined knowledge and inaction may be seen as demonstrable negligence, or as the employer's adoption of the offending conduct and its results, quite as if they had been authorized affirmatively as the employer's policy.

Faragher at 677.

10. Justice Thomas's dissent complains that the defense created in *Ellerth* is vague and poorly defined:

> The Court's holding does guarantee one result: There will be more and more litigation to clarify applicable legal rules in an area in which both practitioners and the courts have long been begging for guidance. It thus truly boggles the mind that the Court can claim that its holding will effect "Congress' intention to promote conciliation rather than litigation in the Title VII context."

Ellerth at 660. What impact do you expect *Ellerth* to have on the federal court docket?

11. The employer's defense in *Ellerth* depends first on the employer establishing "that the employer exercised reasonable care to prevent and correct promptly any sexually harassing behavior." Does this broaden the inquiry to consider the employer's response to sexual harassment generally or just the plaintiff's allegations? Must the employer have a written policy to meet its affirmative defense burden? Will proof of a written policy suffice or is additional evidence required?

12. The second part of the employer's defense is to prove "that the plaintiff employee unreasonably failed to take advantage of any preventive or corrective opportunities provided by the employer or to avoid harm otherwise." The Second Circuit has held that even in cases of co-worker harassment, the employer will be liable if the plaintiff can prove that the company "provided no reasonable avenue for complaint." See Distasio v. Perkin Elmer Corp., 157 F.3d 55 (2d Cir. 1998). In *Distasio,* the court held that plaintiff's allegation that her supervisor threatened her with the loss of her job if she reported a co-worker's harassing behavior, if proven, would render the employer liable for unreported incidents of harassment. What facts must a defendant prove to establish that the plaintiff's failure to take advantage of its policies was unreasonable?

If the employer's policy specifies that the personnel director should receive harassment complaints and the employee who has been harassed by her supervisor complains instead to a supervisor of security, has the employee unreasonably failed to take advantage of the employer's policy or is knowledge imputed to the employer because the supervisor receiving the complaint is an agent of the employer? What if the personnel director is not available at the time the report was made? See Burroughs v. City of Springfield, 163 F.3d 505 (8th Cir. 1998).

13. Consider the facts in *Ellerth*. On remand, what evidence would you present and arguments would you make on behalf of Ellerth? What evidence would you present and what arguments would you make on behalf of Burlington Industries. Was Ellerth subjected to a "tangible employment action?"

14. Is an employer liable for sexual harassment if an employee complains to her employer that she is being harassed by customers and the employer fails to respond? Suppose a sales representative for a manufacturing concern must regularly deal with a customer's purchasing agent who harasses her. Does her employer have a duty to protect her? How far does this duty reach? Must it cease doing business with the harasser's firm if other methods fail? Alternatively, would this employee have a claim against the purchasing agent's employer if it failed to remedy the problem after notice? Quinn v. Green Tree Credit Corp., 159 F.3d 759 (2d Cir. 1998), held that an employer's duty with respect to controlling harassment by customers is the same as its duty with respect to co-worker harassment — the employer is responsible for sexual harassment in its workplace if it knows or should have known of it unless it can show that it took immediate and appropriate corrective action. See also EEOC v. Sage Realty Co., 507 F. Supp. 599 (S.D.N.Y. 1981) (although the employer encouraged the harassment by requiring the plaintiff to wear a revealing costume). We will further consider the problem of employees whose jobs subject them to harassment by customers in the following section concerning gender discrimination in grooming and dress codes.

Page 671. ***Add at end of the first paragraph in the "Note on Adequate Responses to Sexual Harassment":***

Does *Ellerth* limit the employer's ability to use adequate responses to insulate itself from liability for supervisory harassment? Under *Ellerth* an employer can avoid vicarious liability if it can establish that it promptly took action to correct the harassing behavior and that the employee "unreasonably failed to take advantage of any preventive or corrective opportunities provided by the employer." If the employee has acted reasonably, is the employer vicariously liable for supervisory harassment that occurred prior to her complaining through appropriate channels? See Corcoran v. Shoney's Colonial, 24 F. Supp. 2d 601 (W.D. Va., 1998) (employer may be liable for sexual harassment by supervisor despite immediate investigation and response). In evaluating this issue, consider the following language from the Court's opinion in *Faragher*:

> If the plaintiff unreasonably failed to avail herself of the employer's preventive or remedial apparatus, she should not recover damages that could have been

avoided if she had done so. If the victim could have avoided harm, no liability should be found against the employer who had taken reasonable care, and if damages could reasonably have been mitigated no award against a liable employer should reward a plaintiff for what her own efforts could have avoided.

Faragher, at 688.

Page 673. Add at end of the first paragraph:

Should an employer's failure to investigate a harassment complaint create liability under Title VII, even if the harassment did not in fact occur? See Karibian v. Columbia University, 930 F. Supp. 134 (S.D.N.Y. 1996) (no).

What if the employer fails to take action because the employee who complains about harassment asks the employer to keep her complaint confidential? In Torres v. Pisano, 116 F.3d 625 (2d Cir. 1997), the Second Circuit ruled that the employee's confidentiality request insulated the employer from liability for its failure to act. The Court emphasized that some complaints, such as those alleging harassment of other employees as well, may require the employer to breach the trust of an employee who has requested confidentiality, but found that this was not such a case. Is the Second Circuit's approach to this issue consistent with the Supreme Court's opinions in *Ellerth* and *Faragher*? There may be a difference between liability to the employee who asks that no action be taken and liability to a later victim of the harassment if the complaining person's request is honored and no action is taken.

Page 673. Add at end of the first full paragraph:

The Fourth Circuit reheard *Spicer* en banc, vacated the panel opinion, and reversed the district court, holding that the employer's response was adequate. Spicer v. Virginia, 66 F.3d 705 (4th Cir. 1995). The Tenth Circuit has ruled that an employer's responses that are "reasonably calculated to end the harassment" are adequate to insulate the employer from liability for sexual harassment even if new incidents of harassment occur. See Adler v. Wal-Mart Stores, 144 F.3d 664 (10th Cir. 1998). Other courts also have been similarly sympathetic with employers' attempts to control harassment by co-workers, customers, clients, and anonymous harassers. See e.g. Hirras v. National R.R. Passenger Corp., 95 F.3d 396 (5th Cir. 1996) (by taking complaints seriously, conducting prompt and thorough investigation and referring complaints to law enforcement, railroad responded adequately to complaints about anonymous harassing calls, notes, and spray-painted graffiti even though harasser was never identified); Sanchez v. Alvarado, 101 F.3d 223 (1st Cir. 1996) (consistent investigation and graduated disciplinary response to harassment complaints

C. Gender Discrimination

adequate even though co-worker's harassment not immediately stopped); Blankenship v. Parke Care Cntrs., 123 F.3d 868 (6th Cir. 1997) (same); Folkerson v. Circus Circus Enterprises, 107 F.3d 754 (9th Cir. 1997) (casino not liable for customer's harassment of professional mime because casino took adequate steps to protect mime by warning offensive patrons and by assigning a large male employee to follow her and notify security of problems).

Page 674. Add at end of the second full paragraph:

In Morrow v. Wal-Mart Stores, 152 F.3d 559 (7th Cir. 1998), two male employees complained that they were victims of discriminatory discipline when they were fired for violating the employer's sexual harassment policy. Their claims of discrimination failed because they were unable to establish that the policy was not enforced against female employees.

Another source of rights for public employees who are disciplined for harassment is the Constitution. In Cohen v. San Bernardino Valley College, 92 F.3d 968 (9th Cir. 1996), the college's harassment policy prohibiting conduct that has the "effect of unreasonably interfering with an individual's academic performance or creating an intimidating, hostile, or offensive learning environment" was deemed to be unconstitutionally vague as applied to a professor's controversial teaching methods.

Page 674. Add at end of the third full paragraph:

State courts have ruled that an employer who has a reasonable, good faith belief that an employee sexually harassed co-workers has good cause for termination even if the harassment did not actually occur. See Reasonable, Good-Faith Belief That Harassment Occurred Is Defense to Alleged Harasser's Wrongful-Discharge Claim, 153 LRR 232 (10/21/96). The Eighth Circuit, in Freeman v. Bechtel Constr. Co., 87 F.3d 1029 (8th Cir. 1996), ruled that male supervisors disciplined for making or condoning sexually harassing remarks did not state a claim of outrage even though they alleged that their employer had serious doubts about the truthfulness of the harassment complaint.

Page 682. Add at end of carryover paragraph:

See also Charles R. Calleros, Title VII and the First Amendment: Content-Neutral Regulation, Disparate Impact, and the "Reasonable Person," 58 Ohio St. L.J. 1217 (1997).

3.   Grooming and Dress Codes

Page 686.   Add at end of carryover paragraph:

Courts continue to hold that different hair length standards for men and women do not violate Title VII. See Tavora v. New York Mercantile Exchange, 101 F.3d 907 (2d Cir. 1996); Harper v. Blockbuster Entertainment Corp., 139 F.3d 1385 (11th Cir. 1998).

Page 687.   Insert before Craft:

Different standards of dress for men and women (e.g. "dress" clothes versus casual) do not violate Title VII unless members of both sexes are performing the same work. See Lowe v. Angelo's Italian Foods, 87 F.3d 1170 (10th Cir. 1996).

Page 694.   Add new Note 12A:

12A. Mary Anne C. Case, Disaggregating Gender from Sex and Sexual Orientation: The Effeminate Man in the Law and Feminist Jurisprudence, 105 Yale L.J. 1, 68-69 (1995), writes:

> Put quite tendentiously, my contention in pressing quite strongly the claim that sex-specific clothing regulations constitute disparate treatment of a sort prohibited by Title VII is that the world will not be safe for women in frilly pink dresses — they will not, for example, generally be as respected as either men or women in gray flannel suits — unless and until it is made safe for men in dresses as well. Rather than eliminate feminine styles, in clothing and elsewhere, I would prefer to enable them to be more generally valued. While I do not approve and do not mean to encourage the societal tendency to devalue most things limited to women and to value them only insofar as men feel free to engage in them, I do note it, as have many scholars and commentators. In light of this tendency, it seems that one of the most effective ways to improve the value of something coded feminine — whether something as serious as being the primary caregiver for one's child or as seemingly trivial and frivolous as wearing a dress, makeup, or jewelry — is to make it accessible to and acceptable in men. This certainly has, as noted above, been the approach of those seeking to integrate pink-collar ghettos in the workplace, and it is part of my strategy here. Unlike the strategies of many of those promoting the integration of pink-collar ghettos, however, the disparate treatment half of the approach outlined here would only protect, not necessarily encourage, men who engage in behavior coded feminine. At the very least, I would contend, the law should place no obstacle, such as, for example, that posed by ordinances criminalizing cross-dressing, in the way of men who choose to manifest such stereotypically feminine behavior.

C. Gender Discrimination

Page 695. Add new Note 17 after carryover Note 16:

17. Professor Katharine T. Bartlett suggests that community norms concerning dress and appearance cannot be fully removed from the process of furthering workplace equality:

The example of judicial reliance on community norms on which this essay focuses concerns employer dress and appearance requirements. Employers have traditionally assumed substantial prerogatives with respect to the dress and appearance of their employees, imposing burdens on women that are different from those imposed on men. For example, women may be required to wear skirts of a certain length or high-heeled shoes, to conform to different weight criteria than men, or to wear makeup. They may be fired if they have unladylike facial hair or if they wear their hair in a style that may offend customers. They may be required to have sexually alluring figures or to wear sexually provocative clothing, or they may be made to downplay their sexuality. Men, in turn, may be required to wear ties or to keep their hair cut short, or may be prohibited from wearing "women's" jewelry. These requirements pose a special challenge to conventional equality concepts and illustrate especially well the difficulties of rooting out workplace rules and practices that are based on well-settled community norms.

For the most part, courts have rationalized dress and appearance requirements by reference, directly or indirectly, to community norms. Based on these norms, courts may excuse dress and appearance requirements they deem trivial in their impact on employees, or neutral in affecting men and women alike, or essential to the employer's lawful business objectives. These rationalizations have been criticized by scholars, who argue that reliance on community norms constitutes an acceptance or legitimation of the very gender stereotypes that Title VII was established to eliminate. The proposed solution is that community norms be put off limits as a basis for justifying discriminatory standards and that mandatory dress and appearance codes be found unlawful under Title VII.

In this essay I study both the judicial rationales and the scholarly criticisms thereof, agreeing with critics that community norms are too discriminatory to provide a satisfactory benchmark for defining workplace equality, but also questioning the usual implications of this critique. Critics assume that it is possible, and desirable, to evaluate dress and appearance rules without regard to the norms and expectations of the community — that is, according to stable or universal versions of equality that are uninfected by community norms. I question this assumption, arguing that equality, no less than other legal concepts, cannot transcend the norms of the community that has produced it. I argue, further, that eliminating dress and appearance discrimination against women in the workplace is not as simple a matter as the critics suggest. . . . [I]n evaluating dress and appearance codes, my focus is . . . on whether . . . they further gender-based disadvantage in the workplace. Because what constitutes disadvantage, as well as what it takes to reduce that disadvantage and even what reducing disadvantage means, can only be determined in context, in relation to a particular set of circumstances, I conclude that the evaluation of equality claims under Title VII requires more, not less, attention to community norms. . . .

... The law shapes, and is shaped by, community norms, in an ongoing series of negotiations over form and function, over ideals and reality, and over difference, disadvantage, and the difference between the two. In this process of
negotiation, only those versions of equality that incorporate past understand-
ings, as well as new insights, will be stable enough to form the basis of even better future versions. Viewing community norms as a central part of this process
rather than as an evil that can or should be ignored reflects this premise.

Only Girls Wear Barrettes: Dress and Appearance Standards, Community
Norms, and Workplace Equality, 92 Mich. L. Rev. 2541 (1994).

18. Professor Mark Linder has detailed how dress codes requiring women
to wear heels endanger women's health as well as their right to equality in the
workplace. See Smart Women, Stupid Shoes, and Cynical Employers: The
Unlawfulness and Adverse Health Consequences of Sexually Discriminatory
Workplace Footwear Requirements for Female Employees, 22 J. Corp. L. 295
(1997).

4. Sexual Orientation

Page 700. Add at end of carryover paragraph:

Mary Anne C. Case, Disaggregating Gender from Sex and Sexual Orientation: The Effeminate Man in the Law and Feminist Jurisprudence, 105 Yale
L.J. 1, 2-3 (1995), summarizes the problem:

> The word "gender" has come to be used synonymously with the word "sex" in
> the law of discrimination. In women's studies and related disciplines, however,
> the two terms have long had distinct meanings, with gender being to sex what
> masculine and feminine are to male and female. Were that distinct meaning of
> gender to be recaptured in the law, great gains both in analytic clarity and in
> human liberty and equality might well result. For, as things now stand, the con-
> cept of gender has been imperfectly disaggregated in the law from sex on the
> one hand and sexual orientation on the other. Sex and orientation exert the fol-
> lowing differential pull on gender in current life and law: When individuals di-
> verge from the gender expectations for their sex — when a woman displays mas-
> culine characteristics or a man feminine ones — discrimination against her is
> now treated as sex discrimination while his behavior is generally viewed as a
> marker for homosexual orientation and may not receive protection from dis-
> crimination. This is most apparent from a comparison of *Price Waterhouse v.*
> *Hopkins* ... with cases upholding an employer's right to fire or not to hire males
> specifically because they were deemed "effeminate."
>   This differential treatment has important implications for feminist theory.
> It marks the continuing devaluation, in life and in law, of qualities deemed

feminine. The man who exhibits feminine qualities is doubly despised, for manifesting the disfavored qualities and for descending from his masculine gender privilege to do so. The masculine woman is today more readily accepted. Wanting to be masculine is understandable; it can be a step up for a woman, and the qualities associated with masculinity are also associated with success.

We are in danger of substituting for prohibited sex discrimination a still acceptable gender discrimination, that is to say, discrimination against the stereotypically feminine, especially when manifested by men, but also when manifested by women. Ann Hopkins, I fear, may have been protected only because of the doubleness of her bind: It was nearly impossible for her to be both as masculine as the job required and as feminine as gender stereotypes require. But the Supreme Court seems to have had no trouble with the masculine half of Hopkins's double bind; there is little indication, for example, that the Court would have found it to be sex discrimination if a prospective accounting partner had instead been told to remove her makeup and jewelry and to go to assertiveness training class instead of charm school.

Do you agree? Professor Case recognizes the irony that "gender" has come to be used as interchangeable with "sex" in legal literature largely as the result of now-Justice Ruth Bader Ginsburg's work in challenging sex discrimination. Further, the most prominent other recent effort to return to "sex" as opposed to "gender" is by Richard A. Epstein, in Gender Is for Nouns, 41 DePaul L. Rev. 981 (1992), scarcely an admirer of antidiscrimination laws.

Page 701. Add at end of carryover paragraph:

See also Shahar v Bowers, 114 F.3d 1097 (11th Cir. 1997).

Page 701. Add at end of Note 9:

Able v. U.S. 155 F.3d 628 (2d Cir. 1998) (upholding the "don't ask, don't tell" policy against an equal protection challenge).

Page 701. Add at end of Note 10:

Further, the military's "don't ask don't tell policy" and the presumption that mere admission of homosexuality will lead to homosexual conduct survived not only an equal protection challenge, but also a free speech challenge as well, because members were discharged for presumed conduct, not speech itself. Holmes v. California Army Natl. Guard, 124 F.3d 1126 (9th Cir. 1997).

D. RELIGIOUS DISCRIMINATION

Page 713.   Add at end of carryover paragraph:

For example, in Skorup v. Modern Door Corp., 153 F.3d 512 (7th Cir. 1998), plaintiff, a Roman Catholic, alleged that she would not have been terminated if she were Baptist — the faith of the general manager and several other management employees. "She alleges that Baptist management showed a strong preference to Baptist employees, from hiring to preferential job assignments. However, Skorup does not connect this preference for Baptists to her termination. . . . Additionally, Skorup does not address one of the most powerful pieces of evidence against her position: Stokes, the person responsible for selecting her for termination, is also Roman Catholic."

1.   The Special Duty to Accommodate Employees' Religious Practices

Page 726.   Add new Note 3A:

3A. An employer need not accommodate every practice related to even a bona fide religious belief. The court found that the plaintiff's desire to live in a different town was more personal preference than religious belief even though this requirement made it more inconvenient for the employee to attend religious services. Vetter v. Farmland Indus., 120 F.3d 749 (8th Cir. 1997). Similarly, in Tiano v Dillard Dept. Store, 139 F.3d 679 (9th Cir. 1998), an employer who would not give an employee time off from work during the busy season for a religious pilgrimage was held not to violate Title VII when it fired her for not coming to work. Although the worker had a sincere religious belief, which would qualify for Title VII protection, she did not prove that her beliefs required her to go on the pilgrimage during peak season.

Page 726.   Add at end of Note 5:

See generally, Theresa M. Beiner & John M.A. DiPappa, Hostile Environments and the Religious Employee, 19 U. Ark. Little Rock L.J. 577 (1997).

Page 727.   Add new Note 7A:

7A. In Cowan v. Strafford R-VI School District, 140 F.3d 1153 (8th Cir. 1998), plaintiff sent home with her second graders a "magic rock" along with a note saying that the rock "will always let you know that you can do anything that you set your mind to. To make your rock work, close your eyes, rub it and say to yourself three times, 'I am a special and terrific person, with talents of my own.'" Her principal then told the teachers during a staff meeting that "she was concerned about the perception of the school in the community with regard to teaching New Ageism, and she instructed teachers to avoid magical notions in their teaching. In conjunction with this discussion, she announced a seminar coordinated by a local pastor [and grandfather of one of Cowan's second graders], Reverend Stark, that was devoted to the issue of New Ageism and the infiltration of New Age thinking in the public schools." Id. at 1156. At the end of that school year, Cowan's contract was not renewed. Applying *Price Waterhouse*, a jury found for Cowan, which was affirmed on appeal:

> A plaintiff in a discrimination case under Title VII can proceed under the *Price Waterhouse* mixed motives analysis if an employee first establishes that religion was a motivating factor in the employment decision. Then the burden of persuasion shifts to the defendant, who must show that it would have made the same decision even in the absence of the illegal criteria. A plaintiff is entitled to have her case analyzed under the mixed motives standard if she presents "'evidence of conduct or statements by persons involved in the decision making process that may be viewed as directly reflecting the alleged discriminatory attitude.'"

Id. at 1157. Given the evidence of anti-New Ageism in the community and its effect on the principal "there was sufficient evidence presented at trial for a reasonable jury to conclude that persons involved in the decision-making process were motivated by religious concerns regarding the teaching of New Ageism." Id. at 1158. Judge Hansen concurred only because the defendant failed to raise the issue of whether Cowan made out a prima facie religious discrimination claim. "Cowan has never once suggested that she has a bona fide religious belief relating to magic rocks, much less that her employer knew of such a belief or decided not to renew her contract because of it." Id. at 1160. Isn't Judge Hansen conflating religious discrimination with the duty to reasonably accommodate religious practices and beliefs? Would a better argument for the defendant be that Cowan *was* teaching religion, New Ageism, and that should be the basis of the failure to renew her contract because of the establishment clause of the first amendment?

Page 728. *Add at end of carryover Note 9:*

In Rodriguez v. City of Chicago, 156 F.3d 771 (7th Cir. 1998), plaintiff, a police officer, alleged that the city discriminated against him by refusing to exempt him from an assignment to stand guard outside an abortion clinic.

The court held that the city had satisfied "its duty to accommodate Officer Rodriguez by providing him the opportunity, through the [collective bargaining agreement], to transfer to a district that did not have an abortion clinic with no reduction in his level of pay or benefits." This was a "paradigm" of reasonable accommodation, Chief Judge Posner concurred, saying that "police officers and firefighters have no right under Title VII . . . [to] recuse themselves from having to protect persons of whose activities they disapprove for religious (or any other) reasons." Requiring any accommodation is that it would lead "to the loss of public confidence in governmental protective services if the public knows that its protectors are at liberty to pick any choose whom to protect."

> The public knows that its protectors have a private agenda: everyone does. But it would like to think that they leave that agenda at home when they are on duty — that Jewish policemen protect neo-Nazi demonstrators, that Roman Catholic policemen protect abortion clinics, that Black Muslim policemen protect Christians and Jews, that fundamentalist Christian policemen protect noisy atheists and white-hating Rastifarians, that Mormon policemen protect Scientologists, and that Greek-Orthodox policemen of Serbian ethnicity protect Roman Catholic Croats.

While Judge Posner is obviously correct that we all need and expect police protection for our lawful endeavors, no matter what our religious or political beliefs, must all police officers always be available to provide that protection? Is the reasonable accommodation exception to the general rule that police officers must protect lawful activities, such as abortion clinics, any less justified than its operation as an exception to other kinds of employer policies and rules of general application?

Page 728. Add at end of Note 10:

EEOC v. Ilona of Hungary, 108 F.3d 1569 (7th Cir. 1997). See Karen Engle, The Persistence of Neutrality: The Failure of the Religious Accommodation Provision To Redeem Title VII, 76 Tex. L. Rev. 317, 321 (1997) ("Courts considering claims for religious accommodation, contrary to common belief, have been unable to break out of the neutrality paradigm that is predominant in the other categories. Rather than taking an accommodationist approach, courts in the religion cases either follow . . . an integrationist approach — primarily found in the race and national origin cases — or a separationist approach — most commonly found in the sex cases. This inability of religious accommodation to overcome integrationist and separationist ideology is one of many examples of the dominance of the nondiscrimination-neutrality norm in American law . . .").

D. Religious Discrimination

3. The Constitutionality of Title VII's Treatment of Religion

Page 749. Add new Note 5A:

5A. Two contrary views of whether religious institutions should be able to take religious beliefs and practices into account in hiring have emerged recently. Jane Rutherford, Equality as The Primary Constitutional Value: The Case For Applying Employment Discrimination Laws to Religion, 81 Cornell L. Rev. 1049, 1126-1128 (1996), launches an attack on the entire concept of immunizing religions from antidiscrimination laws:

> The problems of discrimination persist because they are deeply imbedded in our common culture. Law, alone, has been unable to eradicate bias. The only hope is broad scale change in social and cultural values. One part of that culture is a religious heritage that is pervasively discriminatory. Section 702 . . . allows religious groups to discriminate on religious grounds, and courts sometimes permit religious institutions to discriminate on the basis of race, sex, age, or disability. Such Congressional or judicial exceptions to civil rights laws violate the Free Exercise Clause because they limit the rights of minorities, women, the aged, and the disabled to practice their religious beliefs on the same terms as the dominant groups. Church leaders have a greater chance of having their religious views incorporated into religious doctrine because of this access to power. When minorities, women, the aged and the disabled are excluded from religious hierarchies, their views are significantly less likely to be acknowledged. Those excluded from leadership positions are denied the right to participate in their own religion. Some might argue that they should then leave and form their own church. Requiring them to leave the institution creates a kind of "separate but equal" segregation long since condemned in other contexts. It also impinges on their religious freedom and precludes them from having access to powerful institutions that shape moral and social policy. Often it precludes them from participating fully in the larger secular world as well because religion is one of the crucial avenues of access to the marketplace of ideas. Therefore, such discrimination undermines other important constitutional rights such as free speech and the free exercise of religion. The First Amendment should not be permitted to be used as a shield to protect such subordinating conduct.
>
> Nevertheless, applying anti-discrimination laws to religions poses free exercise problems for religious groups. Some fear that empowering the government to enforce civil rights laws against religions would completely dismantle religion. That view puts too little faith in religion, however. It assumes that discrimination is the central tenet and that nothing would be left if religion were forced to treat minorities, women, the aged, and the disabled as equals. Nevertheless, religions do risk intrusions on free exercise rights. Courts faced with these decisions are caught in a dilemma. Any decision intrudes on a free exercise right, either of the religious groups or those excluded. The only solution to the dilemma is to look outside the religion clauses for a principled way to decide. That principle may be found in the primacy of equality.

A contrary view is taken by Robert John Araujo, "The Harvest Is Plentiful, But the Laborers Are Few": Hiring Practices and Religiously Affiliated Universities, 30 U. Rich. L. Rev. 713, 724 (1996), proposing that religiously affiliated schools be able to extend apostolic preference not only to co-religionists but to all other employment candidates who are allied with and supportive of the institution's religiously inspired mission. Such preferential hiring practices could help promote and sustain the diversity that is important to American culture and education.

Page 750. Add at end of Note 9:

In City of Boerne v. Flores, 521 U.S. 507 (1997), the Supreme Court found RFRA unconstitutional as applied to states. However, it has yet to be determined whether RFRA is constitutional as applied to the federal government.

Page 769. Add new Note 1A:

1A. In Killinger v. Samford University, 113 F.3d 196 (11th Cir. 1997), an educational institution was found to qualify for both the religious educational exemption and the owned, supported, controlled or managed by a religious association exemption.

Pages 770–771. Delete the last two paragraphs of Note 6 and add:

In City of Boerne v. Flores, 521 U.S. 507 (1997), the Supreme Court held that RFRA is unconstitutional, at least as applied to the states. The Supreme Court also reasserted that the courts retain the power to determine if Congress has exceeded its authority under the Constitution. Whether RFRA will survive a challenge as to federal actions is unclear.

E. NATIONAL ORIGIN AND ALIENAGE DISCRIMINATION

Page 781. Add to Note 6 at the end of the carryover paragraph:

David Ruiz Cameron, How the Garcia Cousins Lost Their Accents: Understanding the Language of Title VII Decisions Approving English-Only Rules as the Product of Racial Dualism, Latino Invisibility, and Legal Indeterminacy, 10 La Raza L.J. 261, 306 (1998), shows "how judges and parties, by their use of language — phraseology, choice of metaphor, or silence, offer insights into why the bilingual population receives a second-class (if any) form of protected status," and he argues that, "Our courts should recognize and address the inescapable relationship between discriminatory English-only policies and valid national origin discrimination claims under Title VII."

Page 783.   Add at end of Note 11:

In Dawavendewa v. Salt River Project Agric. Improvement & Power Dist., 154 F.3d 1117, 1119 (9th Cir. 1998), plaintiff, a Native-American member of the Hopi tribe, claimed national origin discrimination when he was not considered for a job with a private employer operating a facility on the Navajo reservation. The court had "no trouble concluding that discrimination against Hopis constitutes national origin discrimination under Title VII. Because the different Indian tribes were at one time considered nations [by both the colonizing countries and the United States], and indeed still are to a certain extent, discrimination on the basis of tribal affiliation can give rise to a 'national origin' claim under Title VII." The court then rejected the argument that the §703(i) exemption for tribal enterprises giving preferential treatment to "any individual because he is an Indian living on or near a reservation," applied to the defendant's preference for Navajos over Hopis. "An employment practice of giving preference to members of a particular tribe does not afford preference to an applicant 'because he is an Indian,' but rather because he is a member of 'a particular tribe.' Such a preference is not consistent with the objective of the Indian Preferences exemption. . . . In short, we read the term "because he is an Indian" to mean precisely what it says. The reason for hiring must be because the person is an Indian, not because he is a Navajo, a male Indian, or a member of any other formal subset of the favored class." Id. at 1121-1122.

Page 785.   Add to fifth line after extract before "Korean Air Lines":

McNamara v.

Page 785.   Add to the end of the third line of the third full paragraph:

More recently, the Second Circuit found that alienage discrimination is proscribed by §1981 whether the defendant is a private or public actor. In Anderson v. Conboy, 156 F.3d 167 (2d Cir. 1998), the court first held that § 1981 prohibited alienage discrimination:

> Section 1981 provides in relevant part that "all persons within the jurisdiction of the United States shall have the same right in every State and Territory to make and enforce contracts . . . as is enjoyed by white citizens." The statute's juxtaposition of "all" and "white" suggests that it prohibits race discrimination, while its juxtaposition of "persons" and "citizens" suggests that it prohibits alienage discrimination. A "person" who is denied employment because he or she is not a citizen cannot be said to enjoy the "same right . . . to make and enforce contracts . . . as is enjoyed by white citizens." . . . .
>
> Section 1981 is derived from both Section 1 of the Civil Rights Act of 1866 . . . and Section 16 of the Voting Rights Act of 1870. . . . Because Section 1 of the 1866 Act was addressed only to race discrimination and because its protections extended only to "citizens," any prohibition against alienage discrimination must be derived from Section 16 of the 1870 Act. The 1870 Act was passed pursuant to the Fourteenth Amendment, which was ratified in July 1868. . . . Section 16 of the 1870 Act, a portion of which is identical to what is now 42 U.S.C. § 1981(a), used language similar to that found in Section 1 of the 1866, but with one difference of particular relevance here: rather than protecting "citizens, of every race and color," Section 16 protected "all persons within the jurisdiction of the United States."
>
> The use of "persons" rather than "citizens" was deliberate. Because Section 16 was at least in part based on the Fourteenth Amendment, the change in language reflects the language of that newly enacted Amendment, which extended the country's guarantee of the equal protection of the laws to "any person within its jurisdiction." Moreover, the legislative history of the 1870 Act indicates that the change from "citizens" to "persons" reflected the circumstances motivating the enactment of Section 16. The immediate purpose of Section 16 was to alleviate the plight of Chinese immigrants in California, who were burdened by state laws restricting their ability to work, removing their right to give testimony at trial, and otherwise discouraging them from immigrating to and living in California. . . .
>
> The desire to protect Chinese immigrants from discrimination, however, is as consistent with prohibiting racial discrimination as with prohibiting alienage discrimination. . . . However, other remarks in the legislative record suggest that Congress intended to extend Section 16's protections to groups other than the Chinese. For example, Senator Stewart commented that . . . "we will protect Chinese aliens or any other aliens whom we allow to come here." These statements indicate that, whatever the initial motivation behind the legislation, Section 16 was to apply to all aliens. Because not all aliens were likely to be subjected to race discrimination, one may infer that a prohibition on alienage discrimination was contemplated.
>
> The most convincing evidence of such an intent, however, is the structure of the 1870 Act itself. Section 17 of the 1870 Act . . . provided for criminal sanctions for any person who, under color of law, subjected "any inhabitant of any State or Territory to the deprivation of any right secured or protected by the last preceding section of this act . . . on account of such person being an alien, or

by reason of his color or race, than is prescribed for the punishment of citizens." Although Section 17 is a criminal statute and has no direct application here, it was part of the same bill as Section 16. Moreover, Section 17 by its plain language enforced the specific rights enumerated in Section 16. If, therefore, Section 16 did not prohibit discrimination on the basis of alienage, Section 17, imposing criminal penalties for depriving a person of those specific rights "on account of such person being an alien," would be so anomalous as to make no sense.

Id. at 171-174. Having determined that § 1981 prohibited alienage discrimination by governmental actors, the court then held that the 1991 amendments to § 1981 extended that prohibition to private employers:

> The Civil Rights Act of 1991 amended Section 1981 by predesignating the existing text as Section 1981(a) and by adding subsection (b) and (c). Section 1981(c) provides that "the rights protected by this section are protected against impairment by nongovernmental discrimination and impairment under color of State law." Because . . . Section 1981 already protected the designated rights from alienage-based impairment by state laws, Section 1981(c)'s plain language extends that protection to cover private discrimination affecting those rights on the basis of alienage. Had Congress intended to limit Section 1981(c) to claims of race discrimination, it could easily have drafted the subsection to provide that "the rights protected by this section are protected against impairment by nongovernmental race discrimination." It did not do so, however.

Id. at 128.

Page 791.   *Add after the first full paragraph:*

Anderson v. Conboy, 156 F.3d 167, 180 (2d Cir. 1998), in finding that § 1981 prohibited alienage discrimination by public and private employers, held that such a proscription did not interfere with IRCA.

> Although the protections afforded by the IRCA overlap to some extent with those provided by Section 1981, such an overlap does not constitute a conflict between the two statutes. . . . The only purported conflict that appellees identify is the fact . . . that IRCA expressly exempts "illegal" aliens from coverage whereas Section 1981 does not. Thus, according to appellees, applying Section 1981 to claims of private alienage discrimination would "lead to the absurd result of holding liable under Section 1981 employers who refuse to hire undocumented aliens in order to comply with IRCA Section 1324a." We disagree. If an employer refuses to hire a person because that person is in the country illegally, that employer is discriminating on the basis not of alienage but of noncompliance with federal law.

G. RETALIATION

Page 793.   Add at end of the first full paragraph:

Nevertheless, several circuits have concluded that the amended § 1981 does prohibit retaliation for the post-1991 exercise of a § 1981 right. Hawkins v. 1115 Legal Serv. Care, 163 F.3d 684 (2d Cir. 1998); Andrews v. Lakeshore Rehab. Hosp., 140 F.3d 1405 (11th Cir. 1998); Kim v. Nash Finch Co., 123 F.3d 1046 (8th Cir. 1997).

Page 793.   Add at end of page:

Before looking at the two clauses of § 704(a), it is necessary to note the recent cases that have limited plaintiffs' protection to the more serious forms of retaliation. Melissa A. Essary & Terence D. Friedman, Retaliation Claims Under Title VII, the ADEA, and the ADA: Untouchable Employees, Uncertain Employers, Unresolved Courts, 63 Mo. L. Rev. 115 (1998), describe the range of present authority:

> Some courts have adopted an extremely narrow view of actionable retaliation, holding that the retaliation must involve a "material" or "ultimate" employment decision. In these jurisdictions, conduct which falls short of such characterization renders the plaintiff's prima facie case legally inadequate, and as a result, wide open to a summary judgment motion by the defendant. A second set of courts requires that the adverse conduct be related to the employment and have more than a trivial or insignificant effect on the employment relationship. Yet a third set of courts emphasizes that retaliation can come in "many shapes and sizes"; these courts allow for a wide range of actions constituting retaliation, at least for the purposes of surviving the employer's motion for summary judgment.

Id. at 134 (footnotes omitted).

Mattern v. Eastman Kodak Co., 104 F.3d 702 (5th Cir.), *cert. denied*, 118 S. Ct. 336 (1997), establishes an "ultimate employment decision" restriction on protection against retaliation. In that case, the jury found that plaintiff's fellow employees had become hostile to her after she filed a sexual harassment claim, that her tools had been stolen, that her supervisors came to her home to check on the validity of her illness after she called in sick, and that she had missed a chance for a pay increase and had been placed on "final warning." The court nevertheless held that she had no cause of action for retaliation because none of this amounted to an "ultimate employment action." The middle test is typified by Nelson v. Upsala College, 51 F.3d 383 (3d Cir. 1995), in which the employer's barring plaintiff from defendant's campus was

G. Retaliation

not sufficiently detrimental to plaintiff's job opportunities to be an adverse action prohibited by § 704(a). Nevertheless, the court recognized a shortcoming to the test it espoused. "[I]f an employer physically assaults a former employee or burns down her house in retaliation for the employee having brought a Title VII charge, relief might not be available under Section 704. However, in such cases the former employee could assert a state-law damage claim." Id. at 388.

In Wideman v. Wal-Mart Stores Inc., 141 F.3d 1453 (11th Cir. 1998), the Eleventh Circuit rejected the "ultimate employment action" limitation on a § 704 claim. It wrote:

> There is a circuit split on this issue. While the Eighth Circuit has sided with the Fifth Circuit [decision in *Mattern*], see Ledergerber v. Stangler, 122 F.3d 1142, 1144 (8th Cir. 1997) (only adverse employment actions that "rise to the level of an ultimate employment decision [are] intended to be actionable under Title VII."), the First, Ninth, and Tenth Circuits have all held that Title VII's protection against retaliatory discrimination extends to adverse actions which fall short of ultimate employment decisions. See Wyatt v. City of Boston, 35 F.3d 13, 15-16 (1st Cir. 1994) (stating that actions other than discharge are covered by Title VII's anti-retaliation provision and listing as examples "employer actions such as demotions, disadvantageous transfers or assignment, refusals to promote, unwarranted negative job evaluations and toleration of harassment by other employees.") (internal citations omitted); Yartzoff v. Thomas, 809 F.2d 1371, 1375 (9th Cir. 1987) (holding that such non-ultimate employment decisions as "[t]ransfers of job duties and undeserved performance ratings, if proven, would constitute 'adverse employment decisions' cognizable under' Title VII's anti-retaliation provision"); Berry v. Stevenson Chevrolet, 74 F.3d 980, 984-86 (10th Cir. 1996) (construing Title VII's anti-retaliation provision to reach beyond ultimate employment decisions and protect an employee from a malicious prosecution action brought by former employer). . . .
>
> We join the majority of circuits which have addressed the issue and hold that Title VII's protection against retaliatory discrimination extends to adverse actions which fall short of ultimate employment decisions. The Fifth and Eighth Circuits's contrary position is inconsistent with the plain language of [§ 704(a)]. . . . Moreover, our plain language interpretation . . . is consistent with Title VII's remedial purpose. Permitting employers to discriminate against an employee who files a charge of discrimination so long as the retaliatory discrimination does not constitute an ultimate employment action, could stifle employees' willingness to file charges of discrimination. . . .
>
> To establish the causal relation element of her prima facie case of retaliation, Wideman need only show 'that the protected activity and the adverse action are not wholly unrelated.' . . .

Id. at 1456-57. See also Douglas E. Ray, Title VII Retaliation Cases: Creating a New Protected Class, 58 U. Pitt. L. Rev. 405 (1997).

Page 796.   Add after the carryover paragraph:

In Merritt v. Dillard Paper Co., 120 F.3d 1181 (11th Cir. 1997), the plaintiff was discharged after being accused of sexual harassment. Though he was an adverse witness in the claimant's Title VII action, he was nevertheless protected by the participation clause when he was deposed involuntarily in that lawsuit. His subsequent discharge was retaliation because the company president told him that his testimony had damaged the defendant's case and was the reason for his discharge. The court emphasized that employers could discipline supervisors who were guilty of sex harassment for engaging in such harassment, but not simply for participating in a claimant's law suit.

Page 802. Add at end of Note 2:

Three circuits have held that §706(g)(2)(B) is inapplicable. See McNutt v. Board of Trustees, 141 F.3d 706 (7th Cir. 1998), and the cases cited there.

In Thomas v. National Football Players Assn., 131 F.3d 198 (D.C. Cir. 1998), the court first found that the *McDonnell Douglas* prima facie case standard applied in all retaliation cases. Once, however, the employer satisfies its burden of producing a nondiscriminatory reason,

> The plaintiff may aim to prove that a discriminatory motive was the only basis for the employer's action, or the plaintiff may seek to show that the employer was motivated by both permissible and impermissible motives. . . . Where a plaintiff argues that discriminatory motivation constituted the only basis for the employer's action, the plaintiff may persuade the trier of fact of the pretextual nature of the defendant's asserted reason "either directly by persuading the court that a discriminatory reason more likely motivated the employer or indirectly by showing that the employer's proffered explanation is unworthy of credence." *Burdine.*
>
> Where, on the other hand, the plaintiff argues that the action resulted from mixed motives, a slightly different model operates. A plaintiff asserting mixed motives must persuade the trier of fact by a preponderance of the evidence that unlawful retaliation constituted a substantial factor in the defendant's action. *Price Waterhouse.* When the plaintiff successfully shows that an unlawful motive was a substantial factor in the employer's action, the defendant may seek to prove in response that it would have taken the contested action even absent the discriminatory motive.

Id. at 201-202. In accompanying footnote 1, the court referred to §706(g)(2)(B):

> In 1991, Congress amended Title VII to provide that, in the situation where there is a finding of discriminatory motive and also a finding that the firing would have occurred even absent discrimination, the trial judge has discretion

to grant some limited forms of relief: injunctive or declaratory relief, and attorney's fees, but not damages.

Id. at 203. However, the court did not mention that § 706(g)(2)(B) is expressly limited to violations of § 703(m), which prohibits the use of race, color, religion, sex, or national origin in employment decisions, or that other circuits have held that § 706(g)(2)(B) is inapplicable in retaliation actions. Thus, the court's apparent conclusion that § 706(g)(2)(B) changed the effect of a successful same decision defense in a retaliation action from one negating liability to one merely limiting the available remedies was not carefully considered.

In this approach, the court interpreted Justice O'Connor's use of the term "direct" evidence in *Price Waterhouse* as including circumstantial evidence.

> In our view, Justice O'Connor's invocation of "direct" evidence is not intended to disqualify circumstantial evidence nor to require that the evidence signify without inference. In context, the notion of "direct" evidence in Justice O'Connor's concurrence means only that the evidence marshaled in support of the substantiality of the discriminatory motive must actually relate to the question of discrimination in the particular employment decision, not to the mere existence of other, potentially unrelated, forms of discrimination in the workplace. . . .

Id. at 204.

Page 803.   *Add at end of carryover Note 3:*

As previously discussed, some recent cases hold that the employer's conduct must have resulted in an employee suffering "tangible job consequences," not simply unfair warnings, evaluations and counseling. E.g., Sweeney v. West, 149 F.3d 550 (7th Cir. 1998); Benningfield v. City of Houston, 157 F.3d 369 (5th Cir. 1998); Munday v. Waste Management, Inc., 126 F.3d 239 (4th Cir. 1997). Can this line of cases be squared with the Supreme Court's decision in Robinson v. Shell Oil Co. in Note 9 on p. 804?

Page 803.   *Add at end of Note 4:*

In Douglas v. DynMcDermott Petroleum Operations Co., 144 F.3d 364 (5th Cir. 1998), plaintiff was in-house counsel for the defendant. After receiving an unfavorable performance rating, plaintiff sent her letter responding to the rating to outsiders and attached information she had obtained from confidential personnel records in her role as an attorney. The court found that her opposition conduct was not protected:

> This case presents the question whether an in-house counsel's disclosing informally to third parties information relating to interoffice complaints of discrimination against her constitutes a breach of her professional ethical duties of confidentiality and loyalty, and if so, whether such conduct is protected under Title VII. . . . We hold that, although an attorney's unethical disclosure may constitute opposition to practices made unlawful by Title VII, such conduct is nevertheless unprotected under Title VII (and section 1981) as a matter of law.

Id. at 366. Is an employee who happens to be a lawyer always beyond the pale of § 704(a)? If you had been representing Douglas, how would you have counseled her to proceed if she thought that she had been the victim of discrimination? What if she thought she had experienced retaliation because of how she had handled the complaints of discrimination by other employees which came to her as a part of her job?

Page 804. Add cite to *Robinson v. Shell Oil Co.* in Note 9:

519 U.S. 337 (1997)

H. AGE DISCRIMINATION

4. *Bona Fide Employee Benefit Plans*

Page 813. Add after cite to "29 U.S.C.A. §623(*l*)(3)" in first full paragraph:

Cf. Kalvinskas v. California Inst. of Tech., 96 F.3d 1305 (9th Cir. 1996) (employer violated the ADEA when it offset disability benefits by benefits which an employee could receive only by retiring; the offset essentially forced the employee to retire, and was not within §623(*l*)(3)'s "safe harbor" because the employee was not eligible for benefits until he retired).

5. *Early Retirement Incentive Plans*

Page 814. After first sentence in third paragraph, add footnote callout "***" and accompanying footnote at bottom of page:

H. Age Discrimination

*In Lockheed Corporation v. Spink, 517 U.S. 882 (1996), the Court considered whether amendments to an employer's retirement plan violated ERISA and the ADEA. It held that the ERISA prohibition of certain transactions between the plan and parties in interest did not prohibit conditioning of payment of increased pension benefits on retirees' release of any employment-related claims against the employer. The Court further held that amendments to both ERISA and ADEA in the Omnibus Budget Reconciliation Act of 1986 prohibiting age-based cessations of benefit accruals and age-based reductions in benefit accrual rates did not apply retroactively.

Page 815.   *Add at end of second paragraph:*

However, the statute does not provide any substantive rights; it merely defines the requirements for having an effective waiver. Thus, Ellison v. Premier Salons International, Inc., 164 F.3d 1111 (8th Cir. 1999), held that an early retirement offer to employees may be revoked during the statutory 21-day period the law prescribed for their opportunity to consider the offer. OWBPA did not turn an otherwise revocable offer into an irrevocable one.

Page 815.   *Add at end of page:*

The courts have tended to strictly enforce the requirements of OWBPA for a valid release. American Airlines, Inc. v. Cordoza-Rodriguez, 133 F.3d 111 (1st Cir. 1998) (release invalidated for failure to explicitly advise employees to consult an attorney). Tung v. Terence, Inc., 150 F.3d. 206 (2d Cir. 1998), an approach which was taken by the Supreme Court in its first encounter with the statute.

Page 816.   *Delete first full paragraph and insert the following principal case:*

OUBRE V. ENTERGY OPERATIONS, INC.
118 S. Ct. 838 (1998)

Justice KENNEDY delivered the opinion of the Court.

An employee, as part of a termination agreement, signed a release of all claims against her employer. In consideration, she received severance pay in installments. The release, however, did not comply with specific federal statutory requirements for a release of claims under the Age Discrimination in Employment Act of 1967. After receiving the last payment, the employee brought suit under the ADEA. The employer claims the employee ratified and validated the nonconforming release by retaining the monies paid to secure it. The employer also insists the release bars the action unless, as a precondition to filing suit, the employee tenders back the monies received. We disagree and rule that, as the release did not comply with the statute, it cannot bar the ADEA claim.

I

Petitioner Dolores Oubre worked as a scheduler at a power plant in Killona, Louisiana, run by her employer, respondent Entergy Operations, Inc. In 1994, she received a poor performance rating. Oubre's supervisor met with her on January 17, 1995, and gave her the option of either improving her performance during the coming year or accepting a voluntary arrangement for her severance. She received a packet of information about the severance agreement and had 14 days to consider her options, during which she consulted with attorneys. On January 31, Oubre decided to accept. She signed a release, in which she "agree [d] to waive, settle, release, and discharge any and all claims, demands, damages, actions, or causes of action . . . that I may have against Entergy. . . ." In exchange, she received six installment payments over the next four months, totaling $6,258.

The Older Workers Benefit Protection Act (OWBPA) imposes specific requirements for releases covering ADEA claims. 29 U.S.C. §§ 626(f)(1)(B), (F), (G). In procuring the release, Entergy did not comply with the OWBPA in at least three respects: (1) Entergy did not give Oubre enough time to consider her options. (2) Entergy did not give Oubre seven days after she signed the release to change her mind. And (3) the release made no specific reference to claims under the ADEA.

Oubre filed [suit] alleging constructive discharge on the basis of her age in violation of the ADEA and state law. Oubre has not offered or tried to return the $6,258 to Entergy, nor is it clear she has the means to do so. Entergy moved for summary judgment, claiming Oubre had ratified the defective release by failing to return or offer to return the monies she had received. The District Court agreed and entered summary judgment for Entergy. The Court of Appeals affirmed. . . .

II

The employer rests its case upon general principles of state contract jurisprudence. As the employer recites the rule, contracts tainted by mistake, duress, or even fraud are voidable at the option of the innocent party. See 1 Restatement (Second) of Contracts § 7, and Comment b (1979). The employer maintains, however, that before the innocent party can elect avoidance, she must first tender back any benefits received under the contract. See, e.g., Dreiling v. Home State Life Ins. Co., 515 P.2d 757, 766-767 (Kan. 1973). If she fails to do so within a reasonable time after learning of her rights, the employer contends, she ratifies the contract and so makes it binding. Restatement (Second) of Contracts, supra, §7, Comments d, e. The employer also invokes the doctrine of equitable estoppel. As a rule, equitable estoppel bars a party from shirking the burdens of a voidable transaction for as long as she retains the benefits received under it. See, e.g., Buffum v. Peter Barceloux Co., 289 U.S. 227, 234 (1933) (citing state case law from Indiana and New York). Applying these principles, the employer claims the employee ratified the ineffective release (or faces estoppel) by retaining all the sums paid in consideration of it. The employer, then, relies not upon the execution of the release but upon a later, distinct ratification of its terms.

These general rules may not be as unified as the employer asserts. And in equity, a person suing to rescind a contract, as a rule, is not required to restore the consideration at the very outset of the litigation. See 3 Restatement (Second) of Contracts, supra, §384, and Comment b; Restatement of Restitution §65, Comment d (1936); D. Dobbs, Law of Remedies §4.8, p. 294 (1973). Even if the employer's statement of the general rule requiring tender back before one files suit were correct, it would be unavailing. The rule cited is based simply on the course of negotiation of the parties and the alleged later ratification. The authorities cited do not consider the question raised by statutory standards for releases and a statutory declaration making non-conforming releases ineffective. It is the latter question we confront here.

In 1990, Congress amended the ADEA by passing the OWBPA. The OWBPA provides: "An individual may not waive any right or claim under [the ADEA] unless the waiver is knowing and voluntary. . . . [A] waiver may not be considered knowing and voluntary unless at a minimum" it satisfies certain enumerated requirements, including the three listed above. 29 U.S.C. §626(f)(1).

The statutory command is clear: An employee "may not waive" an ADEA claim unless the waiver or release satisfies the OWBPA's requirements. The policy of the Older Workers Benefit Protection Act is likewise clear from its title: It is designed to protect the rights and benefits of older workers. The OWBPA implements Congress' policy via a strict, unqualified statutory stricture on waivers, and we are bound to take Congress at its word. Congress imposed specific duties on employers who seek releases of certain claims created by statute. Congress delineated these duties with precision and without qualification: An employee "may not waive" an ADEA claim unless the employer complies with the statute. Courts cannot with ease presume ratification of that which Congress forbids.

The OWBPA sets up its own regime for assessing the effect of ADEA waivers, separate and apart from contract law. The statute creates a series of prerequisites for knowing and voluntary waivers and imposes affirmative duties of disclosure and waiting periods. The OWBPA governs the effect under federal law of waivers or releases on ADEA claims and incorporates no exceptions or qualifications. The text of the OWBPA forecloses the employer's defense, notwithstanding how general contract principles would apply to non-ADEA claims.

The rule proposed by the employer would frustrate the statute's practical operation as well as its formal command. In many instances a discharged employee likely will have spent the monies received and will lack the means to tender their return. These realities might tempt employers to risk noncompliance with the OWBPA's waiver provisions, knowing it will be difficult to repay the monies and relying on ratification. We ought not to open the door to an evasion of the statute by this device.

Oubre's cause of action arises under the ADEA, and the release can have no effect on her ADEA claim unless it complies with the OWBPA. In this case, both sides concede the release the employee signed did not comply with the requirements of the OWBPA. Since Oubre's release did not comply with the OWBPA's stringent safeguards, it is unenforceable against her insofar as it purports to waive or release her ADEA claim. As a statutory matter, the release cannot bar her ADEA suit, irrespective of the validity of the contract as to other claims.

In further proceedings in this or other cases, courts may need to inquire whether the employer has claims for restitution, recoupment, or setoff against the employee, and these questions may be complex where a release is effective as to some claims but not as to ADEA claims. We need not decide those issues here, however. It suffices to hold that the release cannot bar the ADEA claim because it does not conform to the statute. Nor did the employee's mere retention of monies amount to a ratification equivalent to a valid release of her ADEA claims, since the retention did not comply with the OWBPA any more than the original release did. The statute governs the effect of the release on ADEA claims, and the employer cannot invoke the employee's failure to tender back as a way of excusing its own failure to comply . . .

Justice BREYER, with whom Justice O'CONNOR joins, concurring.

This case focuses upon a worker who received a payment from her employer and in return promised not to bring an age-discrimination suit. Her promise failed the procedural tests of validity set forth in the OWBPA. I agree with the majority that, because of this procedural failing, the worker is free to bring her age-discrimination suit without "tendering-back" her employer's payment as a precondition. . . .

I write these additional words because I believe it important to specify that the statute need not, and does not, thereby make the worker's procedurally invalid promise totally void, i.e., without any legal effect, say, like a contract the terms of which themselves are contrary to public policy. See 1 Restatement (Second) of Contracts, §7, Comment a; 2 id., §178. Rather, the statute makes the contract that the employer and worker tried to create voidable, like a contract made with an infant, or a contract created through fraud, mistake or duress, which contract the worker may elect either to avoid or to ratify. See 1 id., §7 and Comment b. . . .

That the contract is voidable rather than void may prove important. For example, an absolutely void contract, it is said, "is void as to everybody whose rights would be affected by it if valid." 17A Am. Jur. 2d, Contracts §7, p. 31 (1991). Were a former worker's procedurally invalid promise not to sue absolutely void, might it not become legally possible for an employer to decide to cancel its own reciprocal obligation, say, to pay the worker, or to provide ongoing health benefits — whether or not the worker in question ever intended to bring a lawsuit? It seems most unlikely that Congress, enacting a statute meant to protect workers, would have wanted to create — as a result of an employer's failure to follow the law — any such legal threat to all workers, whether or not they intend to bring suit. To find the contract voidable, rather than void, would offer legal protection against such threats.

At the same time, treating the contract as voidable could permit an employer to recover his own reciprocal payment (or to avoid his reciprocal promise) where doing so seems most fair, namely, where that recovery would not bar the worker from bringing suit. Once the worker (who has made the procedurally invalid promise not to sue) brings an age-discrimination suit, he has clearly rejected (avoided) his promise not to sue. As long as there is no "tender-back" precondition, his (invalid) promise will not have barred his suit in conflict with the statute. Once he has sued, however, nothing in the statute prevents his employer from asking for restitution of his reciprocal payment or relief from any ongoing reciprocal obligation. See Restatement of Restitution §47, Comment b (1936) ("A person who transfers something to another believing that the other thereby comes under a duty to perform the terms of a contract . . . is ordinarily entitled to restitution for what he has given if the obligation intended does not arise and if the other does not perform"); Dobbs, supra, at 994 (restitution is often allowed where benefits are conferred under voidable contract). A number of older state cases indicate, for example, that the amount of consideration paid for an invalid release can be deducted from a successful plaintiff's damages award . . .

Justice SCALIA, dissenting.

I agree with Justice THOMAS that the Older Workers Benefit Protection Act (OWBPA), 29 U.S.C. §626(f), does not abrogate the common-law doctrines of "tender back" and ratification. Because no "tender back" was made here, I would affirm the judgment. . . .

Justice THOMAS, with whom Chief Justice REHNQUIST joins, dissenting.

The Older Workers Benefit Protection Act imposes certain minimum requirements that waivers of claims under the Age Discrimination in Employment Act of 1967 must meet in order to be considered "knowing and voluntary." The Court of Appeals held that petitioner had ratified a release of ADEA claims that did not comply with the OWBPA by retaining the benefits she had received in exchange for the release, even after she had become aware of the defect and had decided to sue respondent. The majority does not suggest that the Court of Appeals was incorrect in concluding that petitioner's conduct was sufficient to constitute ratification of the release. Instead, without so much as acknowledging the long-established principle that a statute "must 'speak directly' to the question addressed by the common law" in order to abrogate it, United States v. Texas, 507 U.S. 529, 534 (1993) (quoting Mobil Oil Corp. v. Higginbotham, 436 U.S. 618, 625 (1978)), the Court holds that the OWBPA abrogates both the common-law doctrine of ratification and the doctrine that a party must "tender back" consideration received under a release of legal claims before bringing suit. Because the OWBPA does not address either of these common-law doctrines at all, much less with the clarity necessary to abrogate them, I respectfully dissent. . . .

NOTES:

1. *Oubre* makes clear that releases within OWBPA are subject to very strict requirements. But OWBPA reaches only ADEA claims, not claims under other antidiscrimination statutes. While employers are likely to formulate releases to satisfy OWBPA in order to gain maximum protection, what principles will govern releases of Title VII, ADA, or § 1981 claims?

2. Prior to OWBPA, the courts took different approaches to the question of releases. Some courts have seen two distinct modes of analysis arising in waiver cases. One is the application of normal contract principles. O'Shea v. Commercial Credit Corp., 930 F.2d 358 (4th Cir.); Lancaster v. Buerkle Buick Honda Co., 809 F.2d 539 (8th Cir.). The second is a more rigorous "totality of the circumstances" approach, looking to both the language of the agreement and the circumstances surrounding its signing. Torrez v. Public Serv. Corp., 908 F.2d 687 (10th Cir. 1990); Coventry v. United States Steel, 856 F.2d 514 (3d Cir. 1988) (ADEA); Cirillo v. Arco Chem. Co., 862 F.2d 448 (3d Cir. 1988) (ADEA); Borman v. AT&T Communications, Inc., 875 F.2d 399 (2d Cir.). See also Fortino v. Quasar Co., 950 F.2d 389 (7th Cir. 1991) (upholding release without choosing among the various approaches since the release passed muster under the totality of the circumstances test, which it apparently viewed as the most stringent test). Which approach should govern instances not covered by the OWBPA? See generally Alfred W. Blumrosen, Ruth G. Blumrosen, Marco Carmigani, & Thomas Daly, Downsizing and Employee Rights, 50 Rutgers L. Rev. 943, 1019-20 (1998) (Title VII waivers should be required to meet OWBPA requirements).

3. The majority opinion did not wholly deprive employers of remedies for breach of a release that is not within OWBPA. Rather, it made clear that the employer may be able to recover back the money paid by a claim for "restitution recoupment or setoff." What did the Court mean? Does Justice Breyer's concurrence help?

H. Age Discrimination

Page 817. Add at end of paragraph before Problem 7.3:

See also Judith A. McMorrow, Retirement Incentives in the Twenty First Century: The Move Toward Employer Control of the ADEA, 31 U. Rich. L. Rev. 795 (1997) (arguing that a combination of OWBPA and the increasing use of arbitration has largely removed the operation of the retirement incentive system from public scrutiny).

PART III

ALTERNATIVE APPROACHES TO DISCRIMINATION

Chapter 8

Disability Discrimination

B. PROVING MEMBERSHIP IN THE PROTECTED CLASS

1. The Meaning of "Disability"

Page 834–835. *Delete Notes 6 through 9 and insert the following principal case and notes:*

BRAGDON V. ABBOTT
524 U.S. 624 (1998)

Justice KENNEDY delivered the opinion of the in which STEVENS, SOUTER, GINSBURG, and BREYER, joined.

We address in this case the application of the Americans with Disabilities Act of 1990 (ADA) to persons infected with the human immunodeficiency virus (HIV). We granted certiorari to review, first, whether HIV infection is a disability under the ADA when the infection has not yet progressed to the so-called symptomatic phase; and, second, whether the Court of Appeals, in affirming a grant of summary judgment, cited sufficient material in the record to determine, as a matter of law, that respondent's infection with HIV posed no direct threat to the health and safety of her treating dentist.

I

Respondent Sidney Abbott has been infected with HIV since 1986. When the incidents we recite occurred, her infection had not manifested its most serious symptoms. On September 16, 1994, she went to the office of petitioner Randon Bragdon in Bangor, Maine, for a dental appointment. She disclosed her HIV infection on the patient registration form. Petitioner completed a dental examination, discovered a cavity, and informed respondent of his policy against filling cavities of HIV-infected patients. He offered to perform the work at a hospital with no added fee for his services, though respondent would be responsible for the cost of using the hospital's facilities. Respondent declined.

Respondent sued petitioner under state law and § 302 of the ADA, alleging discrimination on the basis of her disability. The state law claims are not before us. Section 302 of the ADA provides:

> No individual shall be discriminated against on the basis of disability in the full and equal enjoyment of the goods, services, facilities, privileges, advantages, or accommodations of any place of public accommodation by any person who . . . operates a place of public accommodation.

§ 12182(a). The term "public accommodation" is defined to include the "professional office of a health care provider." § 12181(7)(F).

A later subsection qualifies the mandate not to discriminate. It provides:

> Nothing in this subchapter shall require an entity to permit an individual to participate in or benefit from the goods, services, facilities, privileges, advantages and accommodations of such entity where such individual poses a direct threat to the health or safety of others.

§ 12182(b)(3). [On cross-motions for summary judgment, the] District Court ruled in favor of the plaintiffs, holding that respondent's HIV infection satisfied the ADA's definition of disability. The court held further that petitioner raised no genuine issue of material fact as to whether respondent's HIV infection would have posed a direct threat to the health or safety of others during the course of a dental treatment. . . .

The Court of Appeals affirmed. It held respondent's HIV infection was a disability under the ADA, even though her infection had not yet progressed to the symptomatic stage. The Court of Appeals also agreed that treating the respondent in petitioner's office would not have posed a direct threat to the health and safety of others. . . .

II

We first review the ruling that respondent's HIV infection constituted a disability under the ADA. The statute defines disability as:

(A) a physical or mental impairment that substantially limits one or more of the major life activities of such individual;

(B) a record of such an impairment; or

(C) being regarded as having such impairment.

§ 12102(2). We hold respondent's HIV infection was a disability under subsection (A) of the definitional section of the statute. In light of this conclusion, we need not consider the applicability of subsections (B) or (C).

Our consideration of subsection (A) of the definition proceeds in three steps. First, we consider whether respondent's HIV infection was a physical impairment. Second, we identify the life activity upon which respondent relies (reproduction and child bearing) and determine whether it constitutes a major life activity under the ADA. Third, tying the two statutory phrases together, we ask whether the impairment substantially limited the major life activity. In construing the statute, we are informed by interpretations of parallel definitions in previous statutes and the views of various administrative agencies which have faced this interpretive question.

A

The ADA's definition of disability is drawn almost verbatim from the definition of "handicapped individual" included in the Rehabilitation Act of 1973, and the definition of "handicap" contained in the Fair Housing Amendments Act of 1988. Congress' repetition of a well-established term carries the implication that Congress intended the term to be construed in accordance with pre-existing regulatory interpretations. In this case, Congress did more than suggest this construction; it adopted a specific statutory provision in the ADA directing as follows:

> Except as otherwise provided in this chapter, nothing in this chapter shall be construed to apply a lesser standard than the standards applied under title V of the Rehabilitation Act of 1973 or the regulations issued by Federal agencies pursuant to such title.

42 U.S.C. § 12201(a). The directive requires us to construe the ADA to grant at least as much protection as provided by the regulations implementing the Rehabilitation Act.

1

The first step in the inquiry under subsection (A) requires us to determine whether respondent's condition constituted a physical impairment. The Department of Health, Education and Welfare (HEW) issued the first regulations interpreting the Rehabilitation Act in 1977. The regulations are of particular significance because, at the time, HEW was the agency responsible for coordinating the implementation and enforcement of §504. The HEW regulations, which appear without change in the current regulations issued by the Department of Health and Human Services, define "physical or mental impairment" to mean:

(A) any physiological disorder or condition, cosmetic disfigurement, or anatomical loss affecting one or more of the following body systems: neurological; musculoskeletal; special sense organs; respiratory, including speech organs; cardiovascular; reproductive, digestive, genitourinary; hemic and lymphatic; skin; and endocrine; or

(B) any mental or psychological disorder, such as mental retardation, organic brain syndrome, emotional or mental illness, and specific learning disabilities."

45 CFR §84.3(j)(2)(i) (1997). In issuing these regulations, HEW decided against including a list of disorders constituting physical or mental impairments, out of concern that any specific enumeration might not be comprehensive. 42 Fed. Reg. 22685 (1977), reprinted in 45 CFR pt. 84, App. A, p. 334 (1997). The commentary accompanying the regulations, however, contains a representative list of disorders and conditions constituting physical impairments, including "such diseases and conditions as orthopedic, visual, speech, and hearing impairments, cerebral palsy, epilepsy, muscular dystrophy, multiple sclerosis, cancer, heart disease, diabetes, mental retardation, emotional illness, and . . . drug addiction and alcoholism." Id.

In 1980, the President transferred responsibility for the implementation and enforcement of §504 to the Attorney General. See, e.g., Exec. Order No. 12250, 3 CFR 298 (1981). The regulations issued by the Justice Department, which remain in force to this day, adopted verbatim the HEW definition of physical impairment quoted above. 28 CFR §41.31(a)(1) (1997). In addition, the representative list of diseases and conditions originally relegated to the commentary accompanying the HEW regulations were incorporated into the text of the regulations. Id.

HIV infection is not included in the list of specific disorders constituting physical impairments, in part because HIV was not identified as the cause of AIDS until 1983. HIV infection does fall well within the general definition set forth by the regulations, however.

The disease follows a predictable and, as of today, an unalterable course. Once a person is infected with HIV, the virus invades different cells in the blood and in body tissues. Certain white blood cells, known as helper T-lymphocytes or CD4+ cells, are particularly vulnerable to HIV. The virus attaches to the CD4 receptor site of the target cell and fuses its membrane to the cell's membrane. HIV is a retrovirus, which means it uses an enzyme to convert its own genetic material into a form indistinguishable from the genetic material of the target cell. The virus' genetic material migrates to the cell's nucleus and becomes integrated with the cell's chromosomes. Once integrated, the virus can use the cell's own genetic machinery to replicate itself. Additional copies of the virus are released into the body and infect other cells in turn. [medical citations omitted]

The virus eventually kills the infected host cell. CD4+ cells play a critical role in coordinating the body's immune response system, and the decline in their number causes corresponding deterioration of the body's ability to fight infections from many sources. Tracking the infected individual's CD4+ cell count is one of the most accurate measures of the course of the disease. [medical citations omitted]

The initial stage of HIV infection is known as acute or primary HIV infection. In a typical case, this stage lasts three months. The virus concentrates in the blood. The assault on the immune system is immediate. The victim suffers from a sudden and serious decline in the number of white blood cells. There is no latency period. Mononucleosis-like symptoms often emerge between six days and six weeks after infection, at times accompanied by fever, headache, enlargement of the lymph nodes (lymphadenopathy), muscle pain (myalgia), rash, lethargy, gastrointestinal disorders, and neurological disorders. Usually these symptoms abate within 14 to 21 days. HIV antibodies appear in the bloodstream within 3 weeks; circulating HIV can be detected within 10 weeks. [medical citations omitted]

After the symptoms associated with the initial stage subside, the disease enters what is referred to sometimes as its asymptomatic phase. The term is a misnomer, in some respects, for clinical features persist throughout, including lymphadenopathy, dermatological disorders, oral lesions, and bacterial infections. Although it varies with each individual, in most instances this stage lasts from 7 to 11 years. The virus now tends to concentrate in the lymph nodes, though low levels of the virus continue to appear in the blood. It was once thought the virus became inactive during this period, but it is now known that the relative lack of symptoms is attributable to the virus' migration from the circulatory system into the lymph nodes. The migration reduces the viral presence in other parts of the body, with a corresponding diminution in physical manifestations of the disease. The virus, however, thrives in the lymph nodes, which, as a vital point of the body's immune response system, represents an ideal environment for the infection of other CD4+ cells. [medical citations omitted]

A person is regarded as having AIDS when his or her CD4+ count drops below 200 cells/mm3 of blood or when CD4+ cells comprise less than 14% of his or her total lymphocytes. [medical citations omitted] During this stage, the clinical conditions most often associated with HIV, such as pneumocystis carninii pneumonia, Kaposi's sarcoma, and non-Hodgkins lymphoma, tend to appear. In addition, the general systemic disorders present during all stages of the disease, such as fever, weight loss, fatigue, lesions, nausea, and diarrhea, tend to worsen. In most cases, once the patient's CD4+ count drops below 10 cells/mm3, death soon follows. [medical citations omitted]

In light of the immediacy with which the virus begins to damage the infected person's white blood cells and the severity of the disease, we hold it is an impairment from the moment of infection. As noted earlier, infection with HIV causes immediate abnormalities in a person's blood, and the infected person's white cell count continues to drop throughout the course of the disease, even when the attack is concentrated in the lymph nodes. In light of these facts, HIV infection must be regarded as a physiological disorder with a constant and detrimental effect on the infected person's hemic and lymphatic systems from the moment of infection. HIV infection satisfies the statutory and regulatory definition of a physical impairment during every stage of the disease.

2

The statute is not operative, and the definition not satisfied, unless the impairment affects a major life activity. Respondent's claim throughout this case has been that the HIV infection placed a substantial limitation on her ability to reproduce and to bear children. Given the pervasive, and invariably fatal, course of the disease, its effect on major life activities of many sorts might have been relevant to our inquiry. Respondent and a number of amici make arguments about HIV's profound impact on almost every phase of the infected person's life. In light of these submissions, it may seem legalistic to circumscribe our discussion to the activity of reproduction. We have little doubt that had different parties brought the suit they would have maintained that an HIV infection imposes substantial limitations on other major life activities.

From the outset, however, the case has been treated as one in which reproduction was the major life activity limited by the impairment. It is our practice to decide cases on the grounds raised and considered in the Court of Appeals and included in the question on which we granted certiorari. We ask, then, whether reproduction is a major life activity.

We have little difficulty concluding that it is. As the Court of Appeals held, "the plain meaning of the word 'major' denotes comparative importance" and "suggests that the touchstone for determining an activity's inclusion under the statutory rubric is its significance." Reproduction falls well within the phrase "major life activity." Reproduction and the sexual dynamics surrounding it are central to the life process itself.

While petitioner concedes the importance of reproduction, he claims that Congress intended the ADA only to cover those aspects of a person's life which have a public, economic, or daily character. The argument founders on the statutory language. Nothing in the definition suggests that activities without a public, economic, or daily dimension may somehow be regarded as so unimportant or insignificant as to fall outside the meaning of the word "major." The breadth of the term confounds the attempt to limit its construction in this manner.

As we have noted, the ADA must be construed to be consistent with regulations issued to implement the Rehabilitation Act. Rather than enunciating a general principle for determining what is and is not a major life activity, the Rehabilitation Act regulations instead provide a representative list, defining term to include "functions such as caring for one's self, performing manual tasks, walking, seeing, hearing, speaking, breathing, learning, and working." 45 CFR § 84.3(j)(2)(ii) (1997); 28 CFR § 41.31(b)(2) (1997). As the use of the term "such as" confirms, the list is illustrative, not exhaustive.

These regulations are contrary to petitioner's attempt to limit the meaning of the term "major" to public activities. The inclusion of activities such as caring for one's self and performing manual tasks belies the suggestion that a task must have a public or economic character in order to be a major life activity for purposes of the ADA. On the contrary, the Rehabilitation Act regulations support the inclusion of reproduction as a major life activity, since reproduction could not be regarded as any less important than working and learning. Petitioner advances no credible basis for confining major life activities to those with a public, economic, or daily aspect. In the absence of any reason to reach a contrary conclusion, we agree with the Court of Appeals' determination that reproduction is a major life activity for the purposes of the ADA.

3

The final element of the disability definition in subsection (A) is whether respondent's physical impairment was a substantial limit on the major life activity she asserts. The Rehabilitation Act regulations provide no additional guidance.

Our evaluation of the medical evidence leads us to conclude that respondent's infection substantially limited her ability to reproduce in two independent ways. First, a woman infected with HIV who tries to conceive a child imposes on the man a significant risk of becoming infected. The cumulative results of 13 studies collected in a 1994 textbook on AIDS indicates that 20% of male partners of women with HIV became HIV-positive themselves, with a majority of the studies finding a statistically significant risk of infection. [medical citations omitted]

Second, an infected woman risks infecting her child during gestation and childbirth, i.e., perinatal transmission. Petitioner concedes that women infected with HIV face about a 25% risk of transmitting the virus to their children. Published reports available in 1994 confirm the accuracy of this statistic. [medical citations omitted]

Petitioner points to evidence in the record suggesting that antiretroviral

115

therapy can lower the risk of perinatal transmission to about 8%. [medical citations omitted] The Solicitor General questions the relevance of the 8% figure, pointing to regulatory language requiring the substantiality of a limitation to be assessed without regard to available mitigating measures. We need not resolve this dispute in order to decide this case, however. It cannot be said as a matter of law that an 8% risk of transmitting a dread and fatal disease to one's child does not represent a substantial limitation on reproduction.

The Act addresses substantial limitations on major life activities, not utter inabilities. Conception and childbirth are not impossible for an HIV victim but, without doubt, are dangerous to the public health. This meets the definition of a substantial limitation. The decision to reproduce carries economic and legal consequences as well. There are added costs for antiretroviral therapy, supplemental insurance, and long-term health care for the child who must be examined and, tragic to think, treated for the infection. The laws of some States, moreover, forbid persons infected with HIV from having sex with others, regardless of consent.

In the end, the disability definition does not turn on personal choice. When significant limitations result from the impairment, the definition is met even if the difficulties are not insurmountable. For the statistical and other reasons we have cited, of course, the limitations on reproduction may be insurmountable here. Testimony from the respondent that her HIV infection controlled her decision not to have a child is unchallenged. In the context of reviewing summary judgment, we must take it to be true. Fed. Rule Civ. Proc. 56(e). We agree with the District Court and the Court of Appeals that no triable issue of fact impedes a ruling on the question of statutory coverage. Respondent's HIV infection is a physical impairment which substantially limits a major life activity, as the ADA defines it. In view of our holding, we need not address the second question presented, i.e., whether HIV infection is a per se disability under the ADA.

B

Our holding is confirmed by a consistent course of agency interpretation before and after enactment of the ADA. Every agency to consider the issue under the Rehabilitation Act found statutory coverage for persons with asymptomatic HIV. Responsibility for administering the Rehabilitation Act was not delegated to a single agency, but we need not pause to inquire whether this causes us to withhold deference to agency interpretations under Chevron U.S.A. Inc. v. Natural Resources Defense Council, Inc., 467 U.S. 837, 844 (1984). It is enough to observe that the well-reasoned views of the agencies implementing a statute "constitute a body of experience and informed judgment to which courts and litigants may properly resort for guidance." Skidmore v. Swift & Co., 323 U.S. 134, 139-140 (1944).

B. Proving Membership in the Protected Class

One comprehensive and significant administrative precedent is a 1988 opinion issued by the Office of Legal Counsel of the Department of Justice (OLC) concluding that the Rehabilitation Act "protects symptomatic and asymptomatic HIV-infected individuals against discrimination in any covered program." Application of Section 504 of the Rehabilitation Act to HIV-Infected Individuals, 12 Op. Off. Legal Counsel 264, 264-265 (Sept. 27, 1988) (preliminary print) (footnote omitted). Relying on a letter from Surgeon General C. Everett Koop stating that, "from a purely scientific perspective, persons with HIV are clearly impaired" even during the asymptomatic phase, OLC determined asymptomatic HIV was a physical impairment under the Rehabilitation Act because it constituted a "physiological disorder or condition affecting the hemic and lymphatic systems." Id., at 271 (internal quotation marks omitted). OLC determined further that asymptomatic HIV imposed a substantial limit on the major life activity of reproduction. . . . In addition, OLC indicated that "the life activity of engaging in sexual relations is threatened and probably substantially limited by the contagiousness of the virus. Either consideration was sufficient to render asymptomatic HIV infection a handicap for purposes of the Rehabilitation Act. In the course of its Opinion, OLC considered, and rejected, the contention that the limitation could be discounted as a voluntary response to the infection. The limitation, it reasoned, was the infection's manifest physical effect. Without exception, the other agencies to address the problem before enactment of the ADA reached the same result.

Every court which addressed the issue before the ADA was enacted in July 1990, moreover, concluded that asymptomatic HIV infection satisfied the Rehabilitation Act's definition of a handicap. See e.g. Doe v. Garrett, 903 F.2d 1455, 1457 (11th Cir. 1990), cert. denied, 499 U.S. 904 (1991). We are aware of no instance prior to the enactment of the ADA in which a court or agency ruled that HIV infection was not a handicap under the Rehabilitation Act.

Had Congress done nothing more than copy the Rehabilitation Act definition into the ADA, its action would indicate the new statute should be construed in light of this unwavering line of administrative and judicial interpretation. All indications are that Congress was well aware of the position taken by OLC when enacting the ADA and intended to give that position its active endorsement. H. R. Rep. No. 101-485, pt. 2, p. 52 (1990) (endorsing the analysis and conclusion of the OLC Opinion); id., pt. 3, at 28, n. 18 (same); S. Rep. No. 101-116, pp. 21, 22 (1989) (same). As noted earlier, Congress also incorporated the same definition into the Fair Housing Amendments Act of 1988. See 42 U.S.C. § 3602(h)(1). We find it significant that the implementing regulations issued by the Department of Housing and Urban Development (HUD) construed the definition to include infection with HIV. 54 Fed. Reg. 3232, 3245 (1989) (codified at 24 CFR § 100.201 (1997)). Again the legislative record indicates that Congress intended to ratify HUD's interpretation when it reiterated the same definition in the ADA.

We find the uniformity of the administrative and judicial precedent construing the definition significant. When administrative and judicial interpretations have settled the meaning of an existing statutory provision, repetition of the same language in a new statute indicates, as a general matter, the intent to incorporate its administrative and judicial interpretations as well. See, e.g., Lorillard v. Pons, 434 U.S. 575 (1978). The uniform body of administrative and judicial precedent confirms the conclusion we reach today as the most faithful way to effect the congressional design.

C

Our conclusion is further reinforced by the administrative guidance issued by the Justice Department to implement the public accommodation provisions of Title III of the ADA. As the agency directed by Congress to issue implementing regulations, see 42 U.S.C. § 12186(b), to render technical assistance explaining the responsibilities of covered individuals and institutions, § 12206(c), and to enforce Title III in court, § 12188(b), the Department's views are entitled to deference. See *Chevron*.

The Justice Department's interpretation of the definition of disability is consistent with our analysis. The regulations acknowledge that Congress intended the ADA's definition of disability to be given the same construction as the definition of handicap in the Rehabilitation Act. 28 CFR § 36.103(a) (1997); id., pt. 36, App. B, pp. 608, 609. The regulatory definition developed by HEW to implement the Rehabilitation Act is incorporated verbatim in the ADA regulations. § 36.104. The Justice Department went further, however. It added "HIV infection (symptomatic and asymptomatic)" to the list of disorders constituting a physical impairment. § 36.104(1)(iii). The technical assistance the Department has issued pursuant to 42 U.S.C. § 12206 similarly concludes that persons with asymptomatic HIV infection fall within the ADA's definition of disability. See, e.g., U.S. Dept. of Justice, Civil Rights Division, The Americans with Disabilities Act: Title III Technical Assistance Manual 9 (Nov. 1993). Any other conclusion, the Department reasoned, would contradict Congress' affirmative ratification of the administrative interpretations given previous versions of the same definition. 28 CFR pt. 36, App. B, p. 609, 610 (1997) (citing the OLC Opinion and HUD regulations).

We also draw guidance from the views of the agencies authorized to administer other sections of the ADA. [EEOC, the Attorney General and the Secretary of Transportation] These agencies, too, concluded that HIV infection is a physical impairment under the ADA. Most categorical of all is EEOC's conclusion that "an individual who has HIV infection (including asymptomatic HIV infection) is an individual with a disability." EEOC Interpretive

B. Proving Membership in the Protected Class

Manual § 902.4(c)(1), p. 902-21; accord, id., § 902.2(d), p. 902-14, n. 18. In the EEOC's view, "impairments . . . such as HIV infection, are inherently substantially limiting." 29 CFR pt. 1630, App., p. 350 (1997); EEOC Technical Assistance Manual II-4; EEOC Interpretive Manual § 902.4(c)(1), p. 902-21.

The regulatory authorities we cite are consistent with our holding that HIV infection, even in the so-called asymptomatic phase, is an impairment which substantially limits the major life activity of reproduction.

NOTES

1. The Court's holding that reproduction is a major life activity has significance far beyond the question whether HIV infection is a disability within the meaning of the ADA. Prior to *Bragdon,* the lower courts were split on this question. *Compare* Pacourek v. Inland Steel Co., 858 F. Supp. 1393 (N.D. Ill. 1994) (infertility caused by esphofical reflux is a disability under ADA) *with* Zatarian v. WDSU-Television Inc., 881 F. Supp. 240 (E.D. La. 1995) *aff'd* 79 F.3d 1143 (5th Cir. 1996) (infertility caused by physiological disorder of the reproductive system not a disability because reproduction not a major life activity). The regulations list reproduction among the body systems that, if disordered, meet the definition of "impairment." Reproduction, however, is not specified in § 1630.2(i), which lists examples of major life activities that, when substantially limited by an impairment, constitute disabilities. *Bragdon* adds reproduction to that list, opening the door for disability claims by individuals who suffer from disorders of the reproductive system that cause them to be infertile or that require treatment to improve fertility.

2. After *Bragdon* what other activities are major life activities that define whether an individual is disabled under the ADA? Although acknowledging that the list of major life activities is not exclusive, lower courts have not been willing to add to it. For example, in Reeves v. Johnson Controls, 140 F.3d 144 (2d Cir. 1998), the court did not consider agoraphobia to be disabling although it limited the plaintiff's "everyday mobility" by restricting his ability to cross bridges and overpasses, enter tunnels, and board trains — the court did not consider everyday mobility to be a major life activity. Is this result correct after *Bragdon?* What about the ability to sleep or drive a car or get along with people? Are these major life activities under the ADA? See Soileau v. Guilford of Maine, 105 F.3d 12 (1st Cir. 1997) (discussing "ability to get along with others" as a major life activity). What about the ability to engage in sexual intercourse?

3. *Bragdon* resolves the issue of ADA coverage for *most* individuals who are infected with HIV. Does the decision provide any assistance to HIV-infected plaintiffs who are unable to bear children for reasons other than their HIV infection? What about an HIV-infected woman who had her fallopian tubes

tied prior to her infection or an HIV-infected man who had a vasectomy prior to his infection? Is such an individual "substantially limited" because some time in the future the individual is likely to develop AIDS, a seriously debilitating and often fatal illness? Consider the impact of the following language in the Interpretive Guidance:

> Some impairments may be disabling for particular individuals but not for others, depending on the stage of the disease or disorder, the presence of other impairments that combine to make the impairment disabling or any number of other factors.

29 C.F.R. pt. 1630, app. § 1630.2(j). If this language suggests that such individuals are not covered, what do you make of the language from the Interpretive Guidance that immediately follows: "Other impairments, however, such as HIV infection, are inherently substantially limiting."? Id.

4. Prior to *Bragdon*, employers prevailed in 92% of the ADA cases that reached a final decision. In many of those lawsuits the employer won because the plaintiff did not meet the definition of disabled under the statute. See Majority of ADA Job Suits Fail In Court, 158 LRR 269 (6/29/98). Beyond its specific holding, does *Bragdon* suggest that lower courts have been too restrictive in their interpretation of "disabled"? Notice the extreme deference the Court gives to agency interpretations of the ADA and remember that agency interpretations broadly construe the meaning of "disabled."

5. *Bragdon* expressly states that the Court is not addressing the question "whether HIV infection is a per se disability under the ADA." Nonetheless, could it be argued that sections B and C of the opinion strongly suggest per se coverage for HIV-infected individuals? Does the opinion support an argument that HIV infection is substantially limiting because it restricts an individual's freedom to engage in sexual intercourse? Does the Court's analysis of reproduction as a major life activity suggest that sexual intercourse might be characterized as a major life activity? Does the Court's analysis suggest what *other activities* might be considered "major" within the meaning of the statute?

6. In Ennis v. National Assn. of Business and Educational Radio, Inc., 53 F.3d 55 (4th Cir. 1995), a former employee sued under the ADA alleging discrimination on the basis of her relationship with her HIV-infected son. In considering whether the plaintiff's son had a disability within the meaning of the ADA, the court stated:

> We believe that [§ 3(2) defining "disability"] requires that a finding of disability be made on an individually-individual basis [sic]. The term "disability" is specifically defined, for each of subparts (A), (B), and (C), "with respect to [the] individual" and the individualized focus is reinforced by the requirement that the underlying impairment substantially limit a major life activity of the individual . . . . There is no evidence in the record before us that A.J. is im-

120

paired, to any degree, or that he currently endures any limitation, much less a substantial limitation, on any major life activity. . . . Were we to hold that A.J. was disabled under the ADA, therefore, we would have to conclude that HIV-positive statute is per se a disability. The plain language of the statute, which contemplates case-by-case determinations of whether a given impairment sub-stantially limits a major lie activity . . . simply would not permit this conclusion.

Id. at 59-60. The dissents in *Bragdon* also emphasized the individualized na-ture of the disability determination. Is *Ennis* still good law after *Bragdon*?

7. Justice Ginsburg's concurrence in *Bragdon* addressed coverage under the ADA for HIV-infected individuals:

HIV infection, as the description set out in the Court's opinion documents, has been regarded as a disease limiting life itself. The disease inevitably per-vades life's choices: education, employment, family and financial undertak-ings. It affects the need for and, as this case shows, the ability to obtain health care because of the reaction of others to the impairment. No rational legislator, it seems to me apparent, would require nondiscrimination once symptoms be-come visible but permit discrimination when the disease, though present, is not yet visible. I am therefore satisfied that the statutory and regulatory defini-tions are well met. HIV infection is "a physical . . . impairment that substan-tially limits . . . major life activities," or is so perceived, 42 U.S.C. §§12102(2)(A),(C), including the afflicted individual's family relations, em-ployment potential, and ability to care for herself, see 45 CFR §84.3(j)(2)(ii) (1997); 28 CFR §41.31(b)(2) (1997).

118 S. Ct. at 2213-214. Justice Ginsburg suggests that HIV infection is sub-stantially limiting in part because it will later develop into a seriously debili-tating illness. If this is so, what about an affliction such as multiple sclerosis, which in its early stages can be relatively asymptomatic, but which may ulti-mately seriously impair an individual?

Page 837–838.   *Add at end of "Note on Diseases That Are Controlled or Correctable":*

The courts continue to disagree about whether to follow the EEOC's position that the substantially limiting nature of an impairment should be judged with-out mitigating measures. *Compare* Matczak v. Frankford Candy and Choco-late Co., 136 F.3d 933 (3d Cir. 1997) (EEOC followed; epilepsy); Arnold v. UPS, 136 F.3d 854 (1st Cir. 1998) (same; diabetes); Baert v. Euclid Beverage, 149 F.3d 626 (7th Cir. 1998) (same; diabetes); Holihan v. Lucky Stores, 87 F.3d 362 (9th Cir. 1996) (same), Harris v. H.& W. Contracting Co., 102 F.3d 516 (11th Cir. 1996) (same; Graves Disease) *with* Gilday v. Mecosta County,

124 F.3d 760 (6th Cir. 1997) (EEOC not followed; diabetes); Sutton v. United Airlines, Inc., 130 F.3d 893 (10th Cir. 1997), *cert granted*, 119 S. Ct. 790 (1999) (same; eyesight).

The Fifth Circuit has taken a unique approach to the guidelines, accepting them only with respect to serious impairments and ailments analogous to those mentioned in the guidelines and legislative history such as diabetes, epilepsy, and hearing impairments. See Washington v. HCA Health Servs. of Texas, 152 F.3d 464 (5th Cir. 1998) (considering the substantially limiting affects of Adult Stills Disease in its unmitigated state). *Washington* thus overrules *Coghlan*, which appears in the case book at page 837. The First Circuit in *Arnold*, supra, similarly limited its ruling to diabetes and suggested that a myopic applicant whose vision is correctable with eyeglasses might not be covered. 136 F.3d at 866, n. 10 ("The availability of such a simple, inexpensive remedy, that can provide assured, total and relatively permanent control of all symptoms, would seem to make correctable myopia the kind of 'minor, trivial impairment,' Senate Report at 23, that would not be considered a disability under the ADA").

The Second, Ninth, and Eight Circuits have applied and broadly construed the EEOC's approach to controlled or correctable impairments. In Doane v. City of Omaha, 115 F.3d 624 (8th Cir. 1997), the plaintiff asserted that his total and permanent blindness in one eye rendered him disabled under the ADA:

> His medical experts testified that his brain has learned to work with environmental clues to develop his own sense of depth perception using only one eye and that he has learned to compensate for his loss of peripheral vision by adjusting his head position. His doctor expressed the opinion that Doane is able to function normally because his brain has learned over the years to make subconscious adjustments to compensate for the limitation.

Id. at 627-28. Despite Doane's ability to function normally, the court found him to be substantially limited with respect to the major life activity of seeing:

> The manner in which Doane must sense depth and use peripheral vision is significantly different from the manner in which an average, binocular person performs the same visual activity. Doane's brain has mitigated the effects of his impairment, but our analysis of whether he is disabled does not include consideration of mitigating measures. His personal, subconscious adjustments to the impairment do not take him outside of the protective provisions of the ADA.

Id. at 627-28. Kirkingburg v. Albertson's Inc., 143 F.3d 1228 (9th Cir. 1998), *cert. granted*, 119 S. Ct. 791 (1999), also found a monoculor-visioned person to be disabled under the statute. But see Still v. Freeport-McMoran Inc., 120 F.3d 50 (5th Cir. 1997) (plaintiff failed to show evidence that blindness in one eye is substantially limiting).

B. Proving Membership in the Protected Class

The Second Circuit used similar reasoning in Bartlett v. NYS Bd. of Law Examrs., 156 F.3d 321 (2d Cir. 1998), to conclude that a learning-disabled bar examination applicant was substantially limited. The court concluded that:

> Dr. Bartlett suffers from a lack of automaticity and a phonological processing defect that significantly restricts her ability to identify timely and decode the written word, that is, to read as compared to the manner and conditions under which the average person in the general population can read or learn. Her history of self-accommodations, while allowing her to achieve roughly average reading skills (on some measures) when compared to the general population, "do not take [her] outside the protective provisions of the ADA." [quoting *Doane*]

Id. at 329.

The Supreme Court has granted certiorari in three cases relating to whether individuals whose impairments can be mitigated or corrected are disabled within the meaning of the ADA. *Kirkingburg*, supra, may decide, among other issues, whether monocular vision is a "disability" under the ADA. 119 S. Ct. 791 (1999); *Sutton*, supra, may determine whether an airline pilot with a correctable vision impairment is disabled and whether courts should defer to the EEOC Interpretive Guidance that disabilities should be analyzed in their uncorrected state. 119 S. Ct. 790 (1999); finally, Murphy v. United Parcel Serv., Inc., 141 F.3d 1185 (10th Cir. 1998), *cert. granted*, 119 S. Ct. 790 (1999), may decide whether a mechanic with hypertension should be evaluated with or without his medication in determining whether he is disabled under the ADA. 142 L. Ed.2d 653 (1999). How do you think the Supreme Court should resolve these issues? Why?

Page 846.   Add at end of Note 2:

Should an individual be permitted to recover under the ADA if his impairment is substantially limiting only because he fails to control an otherwise controllable illness such as diabetes or a psychiatric disorder? See Siefken v. Village of Arlington Heights, 65 F.3d 664 (7th Cir. 1995) (no; diabetes) and Van Stan v. Fancy Colours & Co., 125 F.3d 563 (7th Cir. 1997) (no; bi-polar disorder). Is such an individual "disabled" within the meaning of the statute?

In Burroughs v. City of Springfield, 163 F.3d 505 (8th Cir. 1998), summary judgment was affirmed against an uncontrolled diabetic on different grounds. The plaintiff, a police recruit, failed to state a claim under the ADA because "he was capable of performing the job without accommodation, yet he failed on two occasions to keep himself functional and alert on the job." According to the court, Burroughs was a qualified person with a disability whose employer nondiscriminatorily dismissed him for failing to control his disability which resulted in his inability to perform his job. Is this approach consistent with the language of the ADA? What about reasonable accommodation?

Page 848–849. *Delete "Note on Impairments Related to Reproduction."*

Page 851. *Add to "Note on Substantially Limited":*

Does the Supreme Court's opinion in *Bragdon* suggest that courts have been too restrictive in their interpretation of what it means to be "substantially limited" under the ADA? *Bragdon* found substantial limitation based on the psychological impact of HIV on an individual's ability to have sexual relations due to the possibility of infecting others. Note that, under the statute, the determination whether an individual is substantially limited is generally made by comparing the plaintiff's abilities to the general population. When establishing substantial limitations relating to work, however, the regulations specify that the comparison is to "the average person having comparable training, skills, and abilities." 29 C.F.R. § 1630.2(j)(3)(i).

The Seventh and Eleventh Circuits have both indicated that medical conditions that necessitate disabling treatments may be "substantially limiting within the meaning of the ADA." See Gordon v. E.L. Hamm & Assoc. Inc., 100 F.3d 907 (11th Cir. 1996); Christian v. St. Anthony Med. Cntr., 117 F.3d 1051 (7th Cir. 1997).

Page 856. *Add at end of Note 7:*

Addressing allegations of discrimination on the basis of weight, both the Second and the Sixth Circuits have held that plaintiffs claiming perceived disability must establish that the impairment that the defendant allegedly perceived is an impairment as defined by the statute. Andrews v. State of Ohio, 104 F.3d 803 (6th Cir. 1997); Francis v. City of Meriden, 129 F.3d 281 (2d Cir. 1997). The Sixth Circuit concluded:

> The officers have not alleged that Ohio perceives them to have any *impairment.* That is, they have not alleged a weight or fitness status which is other than a mere, indeed possible transitory, physical characteristic; they have not alleged a status which is the result of a physiological condition or otherwise beyond the range of "normal."

Andrews, 104 F.3d at 810.

B. Proving Membership in the Protected Class

Page 857.   Add at end of Note 8:

Harris was vacated in Onishea v. Hopper, 133 F.3d 1377 (11th Cir. 1998).

Page 859.   Add at end of carryover paragraph:

The Supreme Court has granted certiorari in Murphy v. United Parcel Serv., Inc., 141 F.3d 1185 (10th Cir. 1998), to decide, among other questions, whether a genuine dispute of fact exists about whether the employer regarded the plaintiff as disabled. 119 S. Ct. 790 (1999).

2.   The Meaning of "Qualified Individual with a Disability"

*Page 866.   Replace citation to **McNemar** in first paragraph with:*

91 F.3d 610 (3d Cir. 1996).

Page 866.   Add at end of "Note on the Preclusive Effect of SSA Disability Determinations":

The lower courts continue to be divided on this issue. The Supreme Court has granted certiorari in Cleveland v. Policy Mgt. Sys. Corp., 120 F.3d 513 (5th Cir. 1997), on the following issues: (1) whether a plaintiff's application for, or receipt of, disability benefits under the SSA creates a rebuttable presumption that the plaintiff is not "qualified" under the ADA; and (2) if there is no such presumption under the ADA, what weight, if any, should be given to an individual's SSA application or receipt of benefits in determinating whether an individual is "qualified" under the ADA. 119 S. Ct. 39 (1998). How should the Supreme Court resolve these issues?

Academics have also been troubled by this question. See Matthew Diller, Dissonant Disability Policies: The Tensions Between the Americans with Disabilities Act and Federal Disability Benefit Programs, 76 Tex. L.Rev. 1003 (1998) (suggesting "reconciling the two statutory programs by restructuring the disability benefit programs to harmonize them with the ADA"); Jorge M. Leon, Two Hats, One Head: Reconciling Disability Benefits and the Americans With Disabilities Act of 1990, 1997 U. Ill. L.Rev. 1139 (1997) (receipt of benefits for total disability should judicially estop one from pursuing an employment claim under the ADA).

Page 868. *Add at end of the third paragraph of the "Note on Essential Functions":*

The Fifth Circuit has cautioned that a presumption that uninterrupted attendance is an essential job requirement improperly avoids the individualized assessment of accommodations required by the ADA. See Cehrs v. Northeast Ohio Alzheimer's Research Cntr., 155 F.3d 775 (6th Cir. 1998). In *Cehrs,* the court noted that non-disabled employees were regularly granted unpaid medical leave and concluded that this practice raised a question of fact as to the essential nature of regular attendance and the reasonableness of the proposed accommodation of medical leave. See also Haschmann v. Time Warner Entertainment Co., 151 F.3d 591 (7th Cir. 1998) (two to four week leaves of absence reasonable); Criado v. IBM, 145 F.3d 437 (1st Cir. 1998) (second one month leave of absence may constitute a reasonable accommodation).

Page 869. *Add at end of carryover paragraph:*

In Stone v. City of Mount Vernon, 118 F.3d 92 (2d Cir. 1997), the city argued that it could not hire a paraplegic in the fire department's fire alarm bureau because he could not engage in fire fighting or fire-suppression activities. Reversing summary judgment for the city, the Second Circuit ruled that, rather than defer to the department's judgment on essential functions, the court should have considered evidence concerning the actual job functions of fire alarm bureau employees. Id. at 99-100. The court further indicated that, even if it would be an undue hardship to hire five or ten disabled individuals in the bureau, it might not be an undue hardship to hire one. Id. at 101. Essential functions and reasonable accommodation must be evaluated based on current circumstances.

C. PROVING DISABILITY DISCRIMINATION

1. Individual Disparate Treatment

Page 887. *Add at end of carryover Note 9:*

In McNely v. Ocala Star-Banner Corp., 99 F.3d 1068 (11th Cir. 1996), the court adopted a mixed motive approach to the ADA, but did not discuss the application of the 1991 Civil Rights Act. Rather, the court relied on the Supreme Court's interpretation of Title VII in *Price Waterhouse* [reproduced

p. 172]. In Despears v. Milwaukee County, 63 F.3d 635 (7th Cir.1995) [reproduced at p. 941], the Seventh Circuit used a sole cause standard to evaluate a discrimination claim under the ADA. *Despears*, however, concerned discrimination on the basis of alcoholism which is governed by unique statutory language. See Section D.1. of Chapter 8. How should mixed motive cases be treated under the ADA given that Congress did not expressly address the issue in the statute?

Page 891.   Replace citation to **Benson** *in second paragraph with:*

62 F.3d 1108 (8th Cir. 1995).

Page 891.   Add at end of second paragraph:

The Sixth Circuit, in Monette v. EDS Corp., 90 F.3d 1173 (6th Cir. 1996), has taken a different approach than *Benson*. Under *Monette*, the plaintiff bears the burden of showing that he is qualified to perform essential job functions under a proposed accommodation. Id. at 1183. The defendant is required only to establish that such an accommodation would impose an undue hardship. Id. See also Willis v. Conopco, Inc., 108 F.3d 282 (11th Cir. 1997) (criticizing *Borkowski* for merging reasonable accommodation and undue hardship and shifting the burden of proof to the employer). Which approach is more consistent with the ADA?

2.   Systemic Disparate Treatment

Page 898.   Add at end of the carryover "Note on Blanket Exclusions":

In an out-of-court settlement with the Department of Justice, Arizona and North Carolina agreed to end their policies of automatically barring individuals with diabetes from working as school bus drivers. The Department of Justice views such policies as illegal under the ADA. With respect to the federal Department of Transportation regulations prohibiting insulin-dependent diabetics from operating most commercial motor vehicles and buses, the Transportation Equity Act for the 21st Century, enacted in 1998, requires the DOT to reassess its policy and report back to Congress within 18 months. In addition, in 1996 the American Diabetes Association convinced the Federal Aviation Administration to replace its blanket ban on diabetic private pilots with a policy allowing for case-by-case consideration. Two States to End Ban on Hiring of Diabetic Drivers, 158 LRR 466 (8/10/98). See also Rauenhorst v. U.S. Dept. of Transp., 95 F.3d 715 (8th Cir. 1996) (considering commercial driver vision standards as applied to a driver with monocular vision).

The Ninth Circuit has ruled that an employer cannot selectively defer to federal safety regulations. In Kirkingburg v. Albertson's, Inc., 143 F.3d 1228 (9th Cir. 1998), the plaintiff who failed a vision examination for truck driving, obtained a vision waiver from the Federal Highway Administration. Albertson's refused to honor the waiver because "it had a policy of employing only drivers who meet or exceed the minimum DOT standards." The Ninth Circuit held that the company could not reject the waiver. The Supreme Court has granted certiorari in *Kirkingburg* to decide, among other issues, whether an individual with monocular vision is a "qualified" individual under the ADA even though he has failed to meet the minimum vision requirement set out by the DOT. 119 S. Ct. 791 (1999). Should the Supreme Court permit employers to defer to DOT standards that apply blanket restrictions on disabled individuals?

3.   Failing to Make Reasonable Accommodations

Page 909.   Add new Note 11:

11. Does the ADA require an employer to provide reasonable accommodations to an employee who is regarded by the employer to be disabled if the employee is not, in fact, disabled within the meaning of the statute? See Deane v. Pocono Med. Cntr., 142 F.3d 138 (3d Cir. 1998) (en banc) (raising but not reaching the issue).

Page 910.   Add at end of carryover "Note on Knowing That Accommodation is Needed":

Courts continue to struggle with questions about what triggers the employer's obligation to accommodate and to engage in an interactive process with the employee to explore possible accommodations. At least three issues divide the courts: (1) whether an employee must identify a specific reasonable accommodation in order to trigger the employer's obligation to engage in an interactive process; (2) whether the failure to engage in an interactive process violates the ADA even if no reasonable accommodation was available; and (3) who bears the burden of persuasion with respect to the availability of a reasonable accommodation?

In Bultemeyer v. Fort Wayne Community Schools, 100 F.3d 1281, 1285 (7th Cir. 1996), a school system was required to engage in an interactive process with a custodian about reasonable accommodations. The custodian returned to work after an extended leave for serious mental illness and then failed to report to a work assignment. He was fired hours before a letter arrived from his psychiatrist recommending that he work in a "less stressful" school. The employee himself did not ask for an accommodation. See also Woodman v. Runyon, 132 F.3d 1330 (10th Cir. 1997) (interactive process initiated by merely notifying employer of nature of disability and requesting information about reassignment). Other courts, however, have held that, unless the employee suggests a concrete reasonable accommodation, the employer has no obligation to engage in an interactive process to discuss possible accommodations. See e.g. Willis v. Conopco, Inc., 108 F.3d 282 (11th Cir. 1997) (allergic employee's request for reassignment to a "safe work area" insufficient to trigger obligation to engage in interactive process). Which approach is more consistent with the statute?

In *Willis*, the court held that there is no obligation to engage in an interactive process that is independent of the obligation to reasonably accommodate. Accord Barnett v. U.S. Air, Inc., 157 F.3d 744 (9th Cir. 1998). In contrast the Seventh Circuit suggested in Beck v. University of Wisconsin Bd. of Regents, 75 F.3d 1130 (7th Cir. 1996), that failure to engage in the interactive process may result in employer liability whether or not a reasonable accommodation is possible. Which approach is more consistent with the statute?

With respect to burdens of persuasion, see the "Note on Burden of Proof in Disability Cases" at page 888. The issue of what triggers the obligation to accommodate or at least engage in an interactive process is complicated by the fact that only employees who are "qualified" are entitled to accommodation, but whether an employee is "qualified" depends on whether his disability can be accommodated.

Page 914.   Add after first full paragraph:

Providing an employee's preferred accommodation is not required if the accommodation offered by the employer is reasonable. See Keever v. City of Middletown, 145 F.3d 809 (6th Cir. 1998). On the other hand, providing the employee's preferred accommodation does not insulate the employer from liability if that accommodation does not meet the employee's needs and another accommodation is available that would. See Feliberty v. Kemper Corp, 98 F.3d 274 (7th Cir. 1996).

Page 915.   Add at end of "Providing Accommodations That Are Not Required":

If an employer goes beyond what is required under the ADA, does the employer violate the ADA if it stops providing those accommodations? In Holbrook v. City of Alpharetta, 112 F.3d 1522 (11th Cir. 1997), the plaintiff, a police detective, suffered injuries resulting in a vision impairment. For several years, the department accommodated the detective in a variety of ways. The detective sued the department when it stopped accommodations, arguing that the fact that accommodations were provided proved that they were reasonable. The court disagreed, ruling that the city was free to stop providing accommodations that were not required under the statute. Is this result consistent with the statute? Is it good policy? Why? Why not?

Page 917.   Add after second full paragraph:

The Courts have disagreed about whether reassignment is a reasonable accommodation. In Smith v. Midland Brake, Inc., 138 F.3d 1304 (10th Cir.), *reh'g granted*, 158 F.3d 1060 (1998) (en banc), the Tenth Circuit held that an employee whose disability renders him unqualified to perform his current position is not entitled to reassignment to another position. The court interpreted the statute and EEOC Guidelines to require reassignment only when accommodating an employee in his current position is possible but difficult. In contrast, the Seventh Circuit, in Gile v. United Airlines, 95 F.3d 492 (7th Cir. 1996), held that the ADA may require an employer to reassign a disabled employee who cannot perform the essential functions of his job to a vacant position for which he is otherwise qualified. Which approach is more consistent with the ADA? Even if an employer is not required to reassign an employee as a reasonable accommodation, might it be discriminatory to reject the employee's application for employment in a different position for which he is qualified?

The Second and Third Circuits have both ruled that reassignment to a different supervisor to avoid a stressful relationship is not required under the ADA. See Gaul v. Lucent Techs., Inc., 134 F.3d 576 (3d Cir. 1998); Wernick v. Federal Reserve Bank, 91 F.3d 379 (2d Cir. 1996).

Page 918.   Add at end of second full paragraph:

Courts are sympathetic with an employer's need to define some positions as temporary light duty positions to accommodate temporarily disabled or injured employees who ultimately will return to their original positions. See Mengine v. Runyon, 114 F.3d 415 (3d Cir. 1997) (conversion of a temporary light duty position to a permanent job may be a reasonable accommodation but only when the costs are slight and the benefits considerable).

Page 918.   Insert the following new subsection prior to "Accommodations Necessary to Enjoy the Benefits and Privileges of Employment":

Leave as a Reasonable Accommodation.   Although numerous courts have held that regular and timely attendance is an essential function of the job, see p. 868, several courts have concluded that medical leave can be a reasonable accommodation. See Haschmann v. Time Warner Entertainment Co., 151 F.3d 591 (7th Cir. 1998) (two to four week leaves of absence reasonable; position was vacant for many months before employee was hired and after employee was fired); Cehrs v. Northeast Ohio Alzheimer's Research Cntr., 155 F.3d 775 (6th Cir. 1998) (paid or unpaid leave may be a reasonable accommodation under the ADA); Criado v. IBM, 145 F.3d 437 (1st Cir. 1998) (second one month leave of absence may constitute a reasonable accommodation; company's policy of allowing employees up to 52 weeks of paid disability leave defeats undue hardship claim). Indefinite leave, however, is not a reasonable accommodation even if it is unpaid. See Hudson v. MCI Telecommunications Corp., 87 F.3d 1167 (10th Cir. 1996); Rogers v. Int'l Marine Terminals, 87 F.3d 755 (5th Cir. 1996).

4. The Interrelationship Between Disparate Treatment and Reasonable Accommodation Claims

Page 922.   Add new section 4A before section 5:

4A. Segregation

The ADA includes "segregating" disabled individuals in its definitions of discrimination. 42 U.S.C. § 12112(b)(1). In addition, the EEOC's Interpretive Guidance states that "[r]eassignment may not be used to limit, segregate, or otherwise discriminate against employees with disabilities . . . ." 29 C.F.R. pt. 1630, app. § 1630.2(o). In Duda v. Board of Educ., 133 F.3d 1054 (7th Cir. 1998), the court found that the plaintiff stated a claim under the ADA when his employer transferred him to a new location where he worked alone and was ordered not to speak to others.

5. Defending Against Disparate Treatment and Reasonable Accommodation Claims: Undue Hardship and Direct Threat

Page 931.   Add at end of Note 3:

Estate of Mauro v. Borgess Med. Cntr., 137 F.3d 398 (6th Cir. 1998), reached the same conclusion, holding that a surgical technician with HIV was a direct threat to the health and safety of others because his job required that he place his hands in patients' body cavities in the presence of sharp instruments.

Page 931.   Add at end of Note 4 before period:

, vacated as moot, 25 F.3d 1115 (D.C. Cir. 1994)

Page 931.   Add after cite to **Altman** *in second line of Note 5:*

aff'd, 100 F.3d 1054 (2d Cir. 1996),

Page 933.   Add new Notes 11 and 12 before Problem 8.5:

11. In *Bragdon* the Court also determined the appropriate standard for assessing the reasonableness of the defendant's judgment that a plaintiff's disability poses "a direct threat to the health or safety of others" under 42 U.S.C. § 12182(b)(3):

> The existence, or nonexistence, of a significant risk must be determined from the standpoint of the person who refuses the treatment or accommodation, and the risk assessment must be based on medical or other objective evidence. As a health care professional, petitioner had the duty to assess the risk of infection based on the objective, scientific information available to him and others in his profession. His belief that a significant risk existed, even if maintained in good faith, would not relieve him from liability. To use the words of the question presented, petitioner receives no special deference simply because he is a health care professional. It is true that *Arline* reserved "the question whether courts should also defer to the reasonable medical judgments of private physicians on which an employer has relied." At most, this statement reserved the possibility that employers could consult with individual physicians as objective third-party experts. It did not suggest that an individual physician's state of mind could excuse discrimination without regard to the objective reasonableness of his actions.
>
> Our conclusion that courts should assess the objective reasonableness of the views of health care professionals without deferring to their individual judgments does not answer the . . . question . . . whether petitioner's actions were reasonable in light of the available medical evidence. In assessing the reasonableness of petitioner's actions, the views of public health authorities, such as the U.S. Public Health Service, CDC, and the National Institutes of Health, are of special weight and authority. *Arline*; 28 CFR pt. 36, app. B, p. 626 (1997). The views of these organizations are not conclusive, however. A health care professional who disagrees with the prevailing medical consensus may refute it by citing a credible scientific basis for deviating from the accepted norm. See W. Keeton, D. Dobbs, R. Keeton, & D. Owen, Prosser and Keeton on Law of Torts § 32, p. 187 (5th ed. 1984).

118 S.Ct. at 2210-211. Because the record was not fully developed from a factual perspective, the case was remanded.

12. Den Hartog v. Wasatch Academy, 129 F.3d 1076 (10th Cir. 1997), held that an employee's association with a disabled individual was a direct threat and therefore provided a defense to associational discrimination. In *Hartog,* the plaintiff was a boarding school teacher whose son suffered from psychiatric disorders that caused him to engage in threatening behavior towards other boarding school personnel and their families.

D. SPECIAL PROBLEMS OF DISABILITY DISCRIMINATION

1. *Drug or Alcohol Users*

Page 940. Add at end of carryover paragraph:

One commentator has suggested that Congress made a bad policy choice when it decided to exclude current drug users from coverage under the ADA. See Kenneth J. Vanko, In Search of Common Ground: Leveling the Playing Field for Chemically Dependent Workers Under the Americans With Disabilities Act of 1990, 1996 U. Ill. L. Rev. 1257 (1996).

Page 944. Add at end of Note 5:

The Fourth Circuit, in Shafer v. Preston Memorial Hosp. Corp., 107 F.3d 274, 279 (4th Cir., 1997), concluded that the "legislative history reveals that Congress intended to exclude from statutory protection an employee who illegally uses drugs during the weeks and months prior to her discharge, even if the employee is participating in a drug rehabilitation program and is drug-free on the day she is fired."

2. *Medical Examinations and Inquiries*

Page 945. Add at end of first paragraph in subsection 2a:

Medical examinations given after an offer of employment has been made but prior to the commencement of employment need not be job related or consistent with business necessity. Thus, there is no restriction on the scope of such examinations — only on the use to which they are put. Of course, if they are used to exclude an individual because of disability, then the exclusionary criteria must be job related and consistent with business necessity.

See Norman-Bloodsaw v. Lawrence Berkeley Lab., 135 F.3d 1260 (9th Cir. 1998).

Page 947.   Replace citation to* Brumley *in carryover paragraph with:

62 F.3d 277 (8th Cir. 1995)

Page 947.   Add at end of carryover paragraph:

If an employer asks an applicant questions that are unlawful under the ADA and the applicant lies in response to those questions, should she be permitted to sue under the ADA or is she no longer qualified because she lied on the application? See Downs v. Massachusetts Bay Transp. Auth., 13 F. Supp. 2d 130 (D. Mass. 1998).

If an employer asks an applicant questions that are unlawful under the ADA and the applicant is not hired, allegedly because of his or her response to those questions, must the applicant be a qualified disabled individual in order to sue the employer? The Tenth Circuit, relying on the language of § 12112(d)(2), ruled that a non-disabled applicant can sue for violations of this section. See Griffin v. Steeltek, Inc., 160 F.3d 591 (10th Cir. 1998). Is this result correct?

Page 947.   Add at end of second full paragraph:

Similarly, the Ninth Circuit has held that the ADA does not prohibit an employer from requiring an employee who has missed an inordinate number of days of work, to submit to a medical examination, even if the examination seeks to determine whether the individual is disabled, because such an examination is job related and consistent with business necessity. Yin v. California, 95 F.3d 864 (9th Cir. 1996).

Page 948.   Add at end of the carryover paragraph before period:

, *vacated*, 518 U.S. 1014 (1996).

3.   Retaliation and Interference

Page 948.   Add at end of section 3:

The Third Circuit, in Krouse v. American Sterilizer Co., 126 F.3d 494 (3d Cir. 1997) has held that, because the language of the ADA retaliation provision protects "any individual," a plaintiff asserting a retaliation claim under the ADA need not establish that he or she is a qualified individual with a disability.

6.   Health Insurance

Page 957.   Add at end of Note 6:

On appeal, the Sixth Circuit affirmed the district court's decision in *Parker* precluding a Title I claim by the plaintiff. Parker v. Metropolitan Life Ins. Co., 99 F.3d 181 (6th Cir. 1996). That decision, however, was vacated when the court decided to rehear the case en banc. The Title I issue was not addressed by the en banc court. See Parker v. Metropolitan Life Ins. Co., 121 F.3d 1006, 1009 n.2 (6th Cir. 1997) (en banc). In Gonzales v. Garner Food Servs., Inc., 89 F.3d 1523 (11th Cir. 1996) the Eleventh Circuit followed *Parker*, denying ADA coverage under Title I to a former employee whose employer capped disability benefits after learning that he had AIDS. The Third Circuit has disagreed. See Ford v. Schering-Plough Corp., 145 F.3d 601 (3d Cir. 1998), reproduced below.

Page 957.   Insert the following principal case and Notes 1 through 5 before subsection 7:

FORD V. SCHERING-PLOUGH
145 F.3d 601 (3d Cir. 1998)

COWEN, Circuit Judge.

This appeal presents the purely legal question of whether a disparity between disability benefits for mental and physical disabilities violates the Americans with Disabilities Act. The plaintiff-appellant, Colleen Ford, sued her employer, Schering-Plough Corporation (Schering), and the carrier of Schering's group insurance policy, Metropolitan Life Insurance Company (MetLife), alleging that the two-year cap applicable to benefits for mental disabilities, but not for physical disabilities, violates the ADA. . . .

The facts concerning the plaintiff's employment and her disability are not in dispute. Ford was an employee of Schering from 1975 until May of 1992, when she became disabled by virtue of a mental disorder and was unable to continue her employment. While she served as an employee, Ford enrolled in the employee welfare benefits plan offered by Schering through MetLife. The plan provided that benefits for physical disabilities would continue until the disabled employee reached age sixty-five so long as the physical disability persisted. Regarding mental disabilities, however, the plan mandated that benefits cease after two years if the disabled employee was not hospitalized.

Ford found herself in this latter category, suffering from a mental disorder yet not hospitalized and thus ineligible for a continuation of her benefits past the two-year limit. Her benefits expired on Nov. 23, 1994. . . .

III.

Because the facts of this case are not in dispute, our analysis focuses on the legal question of whether the disparity between mental and physical disability benefits violates the ADA and, as a preliminary issue, whether Ford is even eligible to sue under the ADA. We will address Ford's claims under Titles I and III seriatim.

A.

Ford's first claim alleges that the defendants' group insurance plan violates Title I of the ADA because of the disparity in benefits between mental and physical disabilities. Title I of the ADA proscribes discrimination in the terms and conditions of employment and mandates in relevant part:

(a) General rule

No covered entity shall discriminate against a qualified individual with a disability because of the disability of such individual in regard to job application procedures, the hiring, advancement, or discharge of employees, employee compensation, job training, and other terms, conditions, and privileges of employment.

(b) Construction

As used in subsection (a) of this section, the term "discriminate" includes —

. . . .

(2) participating in a contractual or other arrangement or relationship that has the effect of subjecting a covered entity's qualified applicant or employee with a disability to the discrimination prohibited by this subchapter (such relationship includes a relationship with . . . an organization providing *fringe benefits* to an employee of the covered entity[)] . . . .

42 U.S.C. § 12112(a)-(b) (emphasis added). As the plaintiff correctly observes, the defendants' group insurance plan is a fringe benefit of employment at Schering. Ford claims that the defendants violated Title I of the ADA because the mental-physical disparity constitutes discrimination against her on the basis of her disability.

D. Special Problems of Disability Discrimination

I.

Before addressing the merits of Ford's Title I claim, we must first ascertain whether Ford is eligible to file suit under Title I. . . .

Title I of the ADA restricts the ability to sue under its provisions to a "qualified individual with a disability[,]" whose characteristics are defined as follows:

> The term "qualified individual with a disability" means an individual with a disability who, with or without reasonable accommodation, can perform the essential functions of the employment position that such individual holds or desires. For the purposes of this subchapter, consideration shall be given to the employer's judgment as to what functions of a job are essential, and if an employer has prepared a written description before advertising or interviewing applicants for the job, this description shall be considered evidence of the essential functions of the job.

42 U.S.C. § 12111(8). Thus, an individual eligible to sue under Title I of the ADA must be disabled but still able to perform his or her job duties with or without a reasonable accommodation by the employer. Ford, however, admits that she is currently unable to work even with a reasonable accommodation. Indeed, her disabled status is the reason for her desire to receive the disability benefits at issue here.

The defendants-appellees argue that Ford is clearly ineligible to sue under Title I of the ADA because she is currently disabled. . . . Ford illuminates an internal contradiction in the ADA itself, namely the disjunction between the ADA's definition of "qualified individual with a disability" and the rights that the ADA confers. Title I of the ADA prohibits discrimination by employers regarding the "terms, conditions, and privileges" of employment, 42 U.S.C. § 12112(a), including "fringe benefits" such as disability benefits. Id. § 12112(b)(2). Yet, as Ford and the EEOC as amicus argue, restricting eligibility to sue under Title I to individuals who can currently work with or without a reasonable accommodation prevents disabled former employees from suing regarding discrimination in disability benefits. Once an individual becomes disabled and thus eligible for disability benefits, that individual loses the ability to sue under a strict reading of Title I's definition of "qualified individual with a disability" because that individual can no longer work with or without a reasonable accommodation. In order for the rights guaranteed by Title I to be fully effectuated, the definition of "qualified individual with a disability" would have to permit suits under Title I by more than just individuals who are currently able to work with or without reasonable accommodations.

This disjunction between the explicit rights created by Title I of the ADA and the ostensible eligibility standards for filing suit under Title I causes us to view the contents of those requirements as ambiguous rather than as having an unassailable plain meaning. "The plainness or ambiguity of statutory language is determined by reference to the language itself, the specific context

137

in which that language is used, and the broader context of the statute as a whole." Robinson v. Shell Oil Co., 519 U.S. 337 (1997). The locus of the ambiguity is whether the ADA contains a temporal qualifier of the term "qualified individual with a disability[.]" If the putative plaintiff must, at the time of the suit, be employable with or without a reasonable accommodation, then a disabled former employee loses his ability to sue to challenge discriminatory disability benefits. Alternatively, the term "qualified individual with a disability" may include former employees who were once employed with or without reasonable accommodations yet who, at the time of suit, are completely disabled.

The Supreme Court's recent decision in *Robinson*, which concerned the scope of Title VII, contributes to this ambiguity by lending support for interpreting Title I of the ADA to permit suits by disabled individuals against their former employers concerning their disability benefits. Cases interpreting Title VII are relevant to our analysis of the ADA because the ADA is essentially a sibling statute of Title VII. Indeed, the ADA's accompanying House report states that the purpose of the ADA is "to provide civil rights protections for persons with disabilities that are parallel to those available to minorities and women." H.R. Rep. No. 101-485, pt. 3, at 48 (1990). Furthermore, the ADA incorporates by reference several terms defined in Title VII. See 42 U.S.C. § 12111(7) (incorporating Title VII's definitions of "person", "labor organization", etc.).

In *Robinson*, the Supreme Court analyzed whether former employees are allowed to bring suits against their previous employers under Title VII for post-termination retaliation such as negative job references. The Court found that the term "employees" as used in § 704(a) of Title VII was ambiguous regarding its temporal reach, i.e., whether it covered only current employees or encompassed former employees as well. Resolving this ambiguity, the Court held that the term encompassed former employees in order to provide former employees with a legal recourse against post-termination retaliation.

As with the term "employees" in Title VII, the ADA contains an ambiguity concerning the definition of "qualified individual with a disability" because there is no temporal qualifier for that definition. Congress could have restricted the eligibility for plaintiffs under the ADA to *current* employees or could have explicitly broadened the eligibility to include *former* employees. Since Congress did neither but still created rights regarding disability benefits, we are left with an ambiguity in the text of the statute regarding eligibility to sue under Title I.

We resolve this ambiguity by interpreting Title I of the ADA to allow disabled former employees to sue their former employers regarding their disability benefits so as to effectuate the full panoply of rights guaranteed by the ADA. This is in keeping with the ADA's rationale, namely "to provide a clear and comprehensive national mandate for the elimination of discrimination against individuals with disabilities . . . [and] to provide clear, strong, consistent, *enforceable* standards addressing [such] discrimination . . . ." 42 U.S.C.

§ 12101(b)(1)-(2) (emphasis added). Our decision is also in keeping with the Supreme Court's *Robinson* decision, which found that the temporal reach of Title VII encompasses former employees. . . .

By adopting this interpretation, we part ways with the Seventh and Eleventh Circuits, both of which tendered decisions prior to *Robinson*. . . .

In sum, we respectfully disagree with the district court and sister courts of appeals. We find that Title I of the ADA does permit disabled individuals to sue their former employers regarding their disability benefits. We reach this conclusion because the ADA's proscription of discrimination in fringe benefits generates the need for disabled individuals to have legal recourse against such discrimination and exposes the temporal ambiguity in the ADA's definition of "qualified individual with a disability[.]" We resolve this ambiguity in favor of a broad temporal interpretation of "qualified individual with a disability[,]" that disabled former employees, no longer able to work with or without reasonable accommodations, can sue their former employers concerning alleged discrimination in their package of disability benefits. Our impetus for this conclusion also comes from the Supreme Court's *Robinson* decision allowing former employees to sue under Title VII of the Civil Rights Act of 1964.

II.

Having established Ford's eligibility to sue under Title I, we must now ascertain whether she states a claim that survives the defendants' Rule 12(b)(6) motion. Ford essentially claims that the disparity between benefits for mental and physical disabilities violates Title I of the ADA. However, Ford's argument does not support a finding of discrimination under Title I.

While the defendants' insurance plan differentiated between types of disabilities, this is a far cry from a specific disabled employee facing differential treatment due to her disability. Every Schering employee had the opportunity to join the same plan with the same schedule of coverage, meaning that every Schering employee received equal treatment. So long as every employee is offered the same plan regardless of that employee's contemporary or future disability status, then no discrimination has occurred even if the plan offers different coverage for various disabilities. The ADA does not require equal coverage for every type of disability; such a requirement, if it existed, would destabilize the insurance industry in a manner definitely not intended by Congress when passing the ADA.

This analysis is supported by Supreme Court and Third Circuit precedent concerning the Rehabilitation Act of 1973, 29 U.S.C. § 794 (1994), to which we may look for guidance in interpreting the ADA. See Gaul v. Lucent Technologies, Inc., 134 F.3d 576, 580 (3d Cir. 1998). In Alexander v. Choate, 469 U.S. 287 (1985), plaintiffs sued in response to the Tennessee Medicaid program's reduction in the number of inpatient hospital days for which it would pay. The plaintiffs claimed that the reduction would have a disproportionate effect on handicapped individuals since they would require longer inpatient care than non-handicapped individuals. However, the Supreme Court held that the limit on inpatient hospital care was "neutral on its face[ ]" and did not "distinguish between those whose coverage will be reduced and those whose coverage will not on the basis of any test, judgment, or trait that the handicapped as a class are less capable of meeting or less likely of having." According to the Supreme Court, handicapped citizens did not suffer from discrimination because both handicapped and non-handicapped individuals were "subject to the same durational limitation."

Building on *Alexander*, the Supreme Court in Traynor v. Turnage, 485 U.S. 535 (1988), dismissed a challenge to a federal statute precluding the Veterans Administration from granting extensions to a ten-year delimiting period for veterans to claim their benefits if the veterans' disabilities arose from their own willful misconduct, defined by regulations as including alcoholism. The Supreme Court rejected the argument that the statute discriminated against one type of disability, namely alcoholism. "There is nothing in the Rehabilitation Act that requires that any benefit extended to one category of handicapped persons also be extended to all other categories of handicapped persons."

We have likewise held, in the context of the Rehabilitation Act, that a state's medical assistance statute need not treat every disability equally. In Doe v. Colautti, 592 F.2d 704 (3d Cir. 1979), we dismissed a challenge to a Pennsylvania statute that provided unlimited hospitalization for physical illness in a private hospital but restricted hospitalization for mental illness in private mental hospitals. We rejected the argument that the differential level of benefits violated the Rehabilitation Act by noting that, "in the treatment of their physical illnesses, the mentally ill receive the same benefits as everyone else. A mental patient with heart disease, for instance, is as entitled to benefits for treatment of the heart disease as would be a person not mentally ill." Id. at 708. Our holding in Doe is supported by the D.C. Circuit's decision in Modderno v. King, 82 F.3d 1059 (D.C. Cir. 1996), in which the D.C. Circuit rejected a challenge brought by a former spouse of a foreign service officer against the Foreign Service Benefit Plan under the Rehabilitation Act based upon the plan's lower level of benefits for mental illness as compared to physical illness.

Aside from Supreme Court and Third Circuit precedent in the Rehabilitation Act context, claims under the ADA similar to Ford's have been rejected by three courts of appeals in published opinions. While we disagree with the Seventh Circuit's reasoning in [EEOC v. CNA Ins. Cos., 93 F.3d 1039 (7th Cir. 1996)] regarding the plaintiff's eligibility to sue, we agree with its discussion regarding the merits of the plaintiff's claim. In rejecting the plaintiff's challenge to the disparity between benefits for mental and physical illnesses, the Seventh Circuit stated:

> One of those terms, conditions, or privileges of employment may be a pension plan, but there is no claim here that CNA discriminated on the basis of dis-

ability in offering its pension plan to anyone. It did not charge higher prices to disabled people, on the theory that they might require more in benefits. Nor did it vary the terms of its plan depending on whether or not the employee was disabled. All employees — the perfectly healthy, the physically disabled, and the mentally disabled — had a plan that promised them long-term benefits from the onset of disability until age 65 if their problem was physical, and long-term benefits for two years if the problem was mental or nervous. . . .

[The plaintiff] raises a different kind of discrimination claim, more grist for the ERISA mill or the national health care debate than for the ADA. She claims that the plan discriminates against employees who in the future will become disabled due to mental conditions rather than physical conditions; their present dollars (unbeknownst to them) are buying only 24 months of benefits, instead of benefits lasting much longer. However this is dressed up, it is really a claim that benefit plans themselves may not treat mental health conditions less favorably than they treat physical health conditions. Without far stronger language in the ADA supporting this result, we are loath to read into it a rule that has been the subject of vigorous, sometimes contentious, national debate for the last several years. Few, if any, mental health advocates have thought that the result they would like to see has been there all along in the ADA.

CNA. Likewise, in Krauel v. Iowa Methodist Med. Ctr., 95 F.3d 674 (8th Cir. 1996), the Eighth Circuit rejected a challenge under the ADA to an insurance plan that denied coverage for infertility. Analogizing the infertility exclusion to differential benefits for mental and physical illnesses, the Eighth Circuit stated, "Insurance distinctions that apply equally to all insured employees, that is, to individuals with disabilities and to those who are not disabled, do not discriminate on the basis of disability." Finally, the Sixth Circuit in *Parker* [v. Metropolitan Life Ins. Co., 99 F.3d 181 (6th Cir. 1996)] rejected a claim similar to Ford's made against the same defendants as in the instant case. As the Sixth Circuit held, "Because all the employees at Schering-Plough, whether disabled or not, received the same access to the long-term disability plan, neither the defendants nor the plan discriminated between the disabled and the able bodied."

The cases finding no violation of the ADA by a disparity in benefits between mental and physical disabilities are supported by the ADA's legislative history. As the Senate Labor and Human Resources Committee report states:

In addition, employers may not deny health insurance coverage completely to an individual based on the person's diagnosis or disability. For example, while it is permissible for an employer to offer insurance policies that limit coverage for certain procedures or treatments, e.g., only a specified amount per year for mental health coverage, a person who has a mental health condition may not be denied coverage for other conditions such as for a broken leg or for heart surgery because of the existence of the mental health condition. A limitation may be placed on reimbursements for a procedure or the types of drugs or procedures covered[,] e.g., a limit on the number of x-rays or non-coverage of experimental drugs or procedures; but, that limitation must apply to persons with or without disabilities. All people with disabilities must have equal access to the health insurance coverage that is provided by the employer to all employees.

S. Rep. No. 101-116, at 29 (1989).

In addition, legislative history subsequent to the ADA's passage evinces that Congress did not believe that the ADA mandated parity between mental and physical disability benefits. In 1996, the Senate defeated an amendment to the Health Insurance Portability and Accountability Act of 1996, Pub. L. No.104-191, 110 Stat. 1936 (1996) (codified primarily in Titles 18, 26 and 42 of the U.S. Code), which would have mandated parity in insurance coverage for mental and physical illnesses. Such an amendment would have been unnecessary altogether if the ADA already required such parity. See 142 Cong. Rec. S9477-02 (daily ed. Aug. 2, 1996) (statement of Sen. Heflin). Furthermore, Congress then passed the Mental Health Parity Act of 1996, Pub. L. No. 104-204, Title VII, 110 Stat. 2944 (1996) (codified at 29 U.S.C. § 1185a and 42 U.S.C. § 300gg-5), which mandates, *inter alia*, that a health insurance plan containing no annual or lifetime limit for medical benefits cannot have such limits on mental health benefits. Such congressional action reveals both that the ADA does not contain parity requirements and that no parity requirements for mental and physical disability benefits have been enacted subsequent to the ADA.

III.

Ford attempts to buttress her challenge to the disparity between benefits for mental and physical disabilities by pointing to section 501(c) of the ADA, which contains the "safe harbor" provision covering the insurance industry. This section, codified at 42 U.S.C. § 12201(c), reads as follows:

(c) Insurance

Subchapters I through III of this chapter and title IV of this Act shall not be construed to prohibit or restrict —

(1) an insurer, hospital or medical service company, health maintenance organization, or any agent, or entity that administers benefit plans, or similar organizations from underwriting risks, classifying risks, or administering such risks that are based on or not inconsistent with State law; or

(2) a person or organization covered by this chapter from establishing, sponsoring, observing or administering the terms of a bona fide benefit plan that are based on underwriting risks, classifying risks, or administering such risks that are based on or not inconsistent with State law; or

(3) a person or organization covered by this chapter from establishing, sponsoring, observing or administering the terms of a bona fide benefit plan that is not subject to State laws that regulate insurance.

Paragraphs (1), (2), and (3) shall not be used as a subterfuge to evade the purposes of subchapter [sic] I and III of this chapter.

42 U.S.C. § 12201(c). Ford essentially claims that, once she presents a *prima facie* case alleging discrimination in disability benefits, Schering and MetLife must present actuarial data demonstrating that their plan is not a "subterfuge[.]" Hence, according to Ford, the district court erred in granting the defendants' Rule 12(b)(6) motion since the defendants had not offered data justifying the actuarial basis for the disparity in benefits.

Ford's argument must fail, however, since it runs contrary to Supreme Court precedent, ignores our statutory duty regarding insurance regulation and distorts the role of this court. First, Ford's argument that Schering and MetLife must justify their insurance plan contradicts the Supreme Court's interpretation of a provision similar to section 501(c) in the context of the Age Discrimination in Employment Act (ADEA). Prior to Congress's elimination of the term "subterfuge" from the ADEA in 1990, see Older Workers Benefit Protection Act of 1990, the ADEA granted an exemption from the ADEA's prohibition of age discrimination to an employee benefit plan that was not "a subterfuge[.]" 29 U.S.C. § 623(f) (1988). In Public Employees Retirement Sys. of Ohio v. Betts, 492 U.S. 158 (1989), the Supreme Court rejected a challenge to an insurance plan that rendered covered employees ineligible for disability retirement once they reached age sixty. Relying on its decision in United Air Lines, Inc. v. McMann, 434 U.S. 192 (1977), the Supreme Court concluded that the term "subterfuge" must be given its ordinary meaning of "'a scheme, plan, stratagem, or artifice of evasion.'" *Betts*. In addition, the Supreme Court found that requiring an insurance company to justify its coverage scheme had no basis in the statutory language.

The Supreme Court's definition and analysis of the ADEA's use of the term "subterfuge" are applicable to the ADA's use of the term "subterfuge[.]" Congress enacted section 501(c) of the ADA in 1990 while the Supreme Court decided *Betts* in 1989. Congress therefore is presumed to have adopted the Supreme Court's interpretation of "subterfuge" in the ADEA context when Congress enacted the ADA. "Where, as here, Congress adopts a new law incorporating sections of a prior law, Congress normally can be presumed to have had knowledge of the interpretation given to the incorporated law, at least insofar as it affects the new statute." Lorillard v. Pons, 434 U.S. 575, 581 (1978) Accordingly, as the Supreme Court held in the ADEA context, the term "subterfuge" does not require an insurance company to justify its policy coverage after a plaintiff's mere prima facie allegation.

The second reason that Ford's argument must fail is that it ignores our statutory duty under the McCarran-Ferguson Act regarding insurance cases. Pursuant to that Act, "No Act of Congress shall be construed to invalidate, impair, or supersede any law enacted by any State for the purpose of regulating the business of insurance . . . unless such Act specifically relates to the business of insurance . . . ." 15 U.S.C. § 1012(b) (1994). The ADA does not "specifically relate[ ] to the business of insurance[,]" id., and does not mention the term "insurance" in its introductory section entitled "Findings and purpose[.]" See 42 U.S.C. § 12101. Accordingly, we will not construe section 501(c) to require a seismic shift in the insurance business, namely requiring insurers to justify their coverage plans in court after a mere allegation by a plaintiff. This second reason is integrally related to the third reason Ford's argument regarding section 501(c) fails, namely that requiring insurers to justify their coverage plans elevates this court to the position of super-actuary. This court is clearly not equipped to become the watchdog of the insurance business, and it is unclear exactly what actuarial analysis the defendants would have to produce to disprove the charge of "subterfuge[.]" See *Modderno* (noting confusion as to exactly what actuarial data would be sufficient).

IV.

For the above reasons, we will affirm the September 12, 1996, order of the district court dismissing Ford's complaint for failure to state a claim. Unlike the district court, we find that Ford is eligible to sue under Title I. However, Ford fails to state a claim under Titles I . . . and errs in asserting that the "safe harbor" provision of Title V requires insurance companies to justify their coverage plans after a plaintiff's prima facie allegation.

NOTES

1. Is the Third Circuit's argument that the ADA covers former employees persuasive?

2. Courts that have found former employees not to be covered have struggled with the question whether insurance contracts and their terms are covered under Title III as public accommodations. The Circuits are split on this question. *Schering Plough*, in a portion of the opinion not reproduced, concluded that insurance contracts are not public accommodations. Title III provides that:

> No individual shall be discriminated against on the basis of disability in the full and equal enjoyment of the goods, services, facilities, privileges, advantages, or accommodations of any place of public accommodation by any person who owns, leases (or leases to), or operates a place of public accommodation.

D. Special Problems of Disability Discrimination

42 U.S.C. § 12182(a). "Public accommodation" is defined in the statute to include an extensive list of establishments such as "auditorium," "bakery," "laundromat," "museum," "park," "nursery," "food bank," and "gymnasium[ ]" 42 U.S.C. § 12181(7)(D)-(F), (H)-(L). The statute also lists "insurance office. . . . or other service establishment." 42 U.S.C. § 12181(7)(F). The courts in *Schering Plough* and *Parker* found that the plain language of the statute extends coverage only to "places." Because an insurance policy is not a place and employees who receive insurance as a benefit of their employment never go to the insurance provider's office, Title III is not implicated. In Carparts Distrib. Cntr., Inc. v. Automotive Wholesaler's Assn. of New England, Inc., 37 F.3d 12 (1st Cir. 1994), the First Circuit held that Title III is not limited to physical structures. With respect to the inclusion of "travel service" in the list of public accommodations the court noted:

> Many travel services conduct business by telephone or correspondence without requiring their customers to enter an office in order to obtain their services. Likewise, one can easily imagine the existence of other service establishments conducting business by mail and phone without providing facilities for their customers to enter in order to utilize their services. It would be irrational to conclude that persons who enter an office to purchase services are protected by the ADA, but persons who purchase the same services over the telephone or by mail are not. Congress could not have intended such an absurd result.

Id. at 19. Is this argument persuasive? Even if the telephone services provided by establishments who maintain retail offices are covered by Title III, does that mean that businesses that conduct all of their business over the phone and maintain no retail establishment are public accommodations? The argument that Congress could not possibly have meant to leave such service providers and retailers out of the ADA is answered by pointing to the plain language of the statute.

3. Beyond the question whether former employees and insurance contracts are covered under the ADA is the question whether Title I or Title III of the ADA reach the substance of insurance contracts. Department of Justice regulations provide:

> The purpose of the ADA's public accommodations requirements is to ensure accessibility to the goods offered by a public accommodation, not to alter the nature or mix of goods that the public accommodation has typically provided. In other words, a bookstore, for example, must make its facilities and sales operations accessible to individuals with disabilities, but is not required to stock Brailled or large print books. Similarly, a video store must make its facilities and rental operations accessible, but is not required to stock closed-captioned video tapes.

28 C.F.R. pt. 36, app. B, at 640 (1997). But is this section properly analogized to insurance contracts? If so, why would the statute contain the "safe harbor"

provisions concerning insurance? The Dept. of Justice Technical Assistance Manual states that Title III does cover the substance of insurance contracts, see Dept. of Justice, Title III Technical Assistance Manual: Covering Public Accommodations and Commercial Facilities § III-3.11000, at 19 (Nov. 1993) ("Insurance offices . . . may not discriminate on the basis of disability in the sale of insurance contracts or in the terms or conditions of the insurance contracts they offer."). Under *Chevron* courts must defer to agency interpretations, but only if they are consistent with the statute. Is this interpretation consistent with the ADA? Remember that this interpretation is not contained in a regulation. Remember also that the court in *Bragdon* was very deferential to agency interpretations of the ADA. The question whether the ADA reaches the contents of insurance policies also arises under Title I.

4. If former employees are covered and if the ADA reaches the contents of insurance policies, then the question arises whether the distinctions drawn in the policy violate the ADA. This is the central issue raised by Colleen Ford's lawsuit — whether distinctions in her insurance contract between mental and physical disabilities violate the ADA. Do you agree with the Third Circuit's analysis of this issue? Is the court's approach consistent with the EEOC's Interpretive Guidance? It may seem logical to conclude that distinctions between mental and physical conditions in health insurance contracts are not disability-based because both categories encompass conditions that qualify as disabilities along with conditions that do not. Can the same be said, however, of distinctions between coverage of physical and mental conditions in a disability insurance contract? Aren't all of the individuals who seek benefits under such contracts disabled within the meaning of the statute?

5. As noted in the Third Circuit opinion, several circuits have agreed that distinctions between mental and physical disabilities in insurance contracts do not violate the ADA. There is some contrary authority. See Lewis v. Aetna Life Ins. Co., 7 F. Supp. 3d 743 (E.D. Va. 1998). In *Lewis*, the plaintiff suffered from severe depression. Disability benefits for conditions other than physical impairments ended after two years. Benefits for physical impairments continued until the recipient reached age 65. The court refused to grant the employer protection under the safe harbor provision because Virginia state insurance law disallows plans that provide rate differentials that are not based on sound actuarial principles. Because the employer could not support its distinction with actuarial analysis, the plan was not protected by the safe harbor provision and thus violated the ADA.

7. National Labor Relations Act

Page 959. Add at end of second full paragraph:

Courts continue to be divided on the question whether accommodations that interfere with collective bargaining rights are unreasonable, although most courts so hold. *Compare* Eckles v. Conrail, 94 F.3d 1041 (7th Cir. 1996) (ADA does not require disabled individuals to be accommodated by sacrificing collectively bargained seniority rights of other employees); Kralik v. Durbin, 130 F.3d 76 (3d Cir. 1997) (same); Willis v. Pacific Maritime Assn., 162 F.3d 561 (9th Cir. 1998) (accommodation request that directly conflicts with collectively bargained seniority rights of other employees is unreasonable); Feliciano v. State of Rhode Island, 160 F.3d 780 (1st Cir. 1998) (employer's failure to reassign disabled employee to another position in violation of the rights of an individual who received the position under a process outlined in the collective bargaining contract, does not violate the ADA) *with* Aka v. Washington Hosp. Cntr., 116 F.3d 876 (D.C. Cir. 1997) (whether accommodation is required under the ADA depends on specific nature of the requested accommodation and of the business, including the degree to which the accommodation might upset settled expectations created by collective bargaining contract). Note, however, that the contract at issue in *Aka* included an exception to the seniority system permitting reassignment of disabled employees in some circumstances. The D.C. Circuit subsequently reheard *Aka* en banc. The en banc court remanded the case for the district court to determine whether vacant positions existed to which Aka could be reassigned and whether the collective bargaining agreement permitted reassignment. The court declined to reach the question of how to resolve conflicts between the ADA and the collective bargaining agreement because the record did not permit the court to determine whether a conflict existed. Aka v. Washington Hosp. Cntr., 156 F.3d 1284 (D.C. Cir. 1998).

Page 961.   Add after **Reich** *citation in 4th line of last paragraph:*

aff'd, 113 F.3d 1235 (6th Cir. 1997),

PART IV

PROCEDURES AND REMEDIES

Chapter 10

Procedures for Enforcing Antidiscrimination Laws

B. PRIVATE ENFORCEMENT: THE ADMINISTRATIVE PHASE

2. Filing a Timely Charge

Page 1081.   In carryover paragraph, after **Diez** *cite, add:*

See also Lawrence v. Cooper Communities, Inc., 132 F.3d 447 (8th Cir. 1998) (unverified charge information form submitted by employee to EEOC was not "charge" for purposes of Title VII's filing requirement); Schlueter v. Anheuser-Busch, Inc., 132 F.3d 455 (8th Cir. 1998) (EEOC intake questionnaire containing allegations of sex discrimination did not function as a charge of discrimination under ADEA or Title VII).

Page 1081.   Add at end of carryover paragraph:

Cf. Fairchild v. Forma, 147 F.3d 567, 575 (7th Cir. 1998) (an untimely amendment alleging an entirely new theory of recovery does not relate back to a timely-filed original charge).

Page 1093.   Insert in Note 7 before the **Early** *cite:*

Lawrence v. Cooper Communities, Inc., 132 F.3d 447 (8th Cir. 1998); Schlueter v. Anheuser-Busch, Inc., 132 F.3d 455 (8th Cir. 1998);

Page 1093.   Add new Note 8:

8. Armstrong v. Martin Marietta Corp., 93 F.3d 1505 (11th Cir. 1996), addressed the affects of dismissing plaintiffs from an ADEA class action, holding that § 216(b) eliminates the need for claimants who intend to appeal their dismissal to file individual lawsuits while awaiting final judgment.

Page 1102.   Add at end of Note 16:

Draper v. Coeur Rochester, Inc., 147 F.3d 1104 (9th Cir. 1998) (events occurring outside limitations period may be basis for claim so long as they are part of an ongoing unlawful employment practice; alleged hostile work environment may have continued into relevant limitations period).

3.   Filing a Timely Charge: Deferral States

Page 1109–1112.   Delete from first full paragraph on page 1109 to carryover paragraph on page 1112; replace with:

This question reached the Supreme Court in Gilmer v. Interstate/Johnson Lane Corp., 500 U.S. 20 (1991), which upheld an agreement entered into by plaintiff as a condition of employment providing that any dispute would be resolved by arbitration. Plaintiff had attempted to bring an ADEA claim, but was met with a motion to compel arbitration pursuant to the Federal Arbitration Act. He resisted that motion, relying on *Gardner-Denver*. The Court, however, held that the ADEA dispute must be arbitrated. The majority rejected plaintiff's argument that depriving him of his judicial forum was inconsistent with the ADEA. The Court distinguished *Gardner-Denver* on three grounds. First, the arbitrator there had not purported to resolve Title VII claims, but only had decided just cause under the collective bargaining agreement. Second, the plaintiff in *Gardner-Denver* had no control over prosecution of the arbitration because the union presented his grievance. Third, *Gardner-Denver* was not decided under the Federal Arbitration Act. *Gilmer* rejected several frontal attacks on arbitration as a means of deciding ADEA cases. It first dismissed as speculative plaintiff's claim that the arbitral process, governed by the New York Stock Exchange rules, would be biased toward the employer. It then noted that there was no showing that discovery would be inadequate for an ADEA claim under those rules. Additionally, awards would be public so that objections to hidden decisions were inapplicable. Finally, it stressed that arbitrators have the power to award broad equitable relief, and to the extent their remedial powers are deficient, the EEOC remains able to sue the employer. One circuit has since held that *Gilmer*, in effect, overruled *Gardner-Denver*, in that arbitration clauses, even when contained in collective bargaining agreements, bar suit by individual employees. Austin v. Owens-Broadway Glass Container, Inc., 78 F.3d 875 (4th Cir. 1996). The majority of circuit courts, however, have held that *Gardner-Denver* is still good law. They limit *Gilmer* to arbitration where the employee herself, not her union, agrees to arbitration. Johnson v. Bodine Elec. Co., 142 F.3d 363, 367 (7th Cir. 1998) (Title VII); Peterson v. BMI Refractories, 132 F.3d 1405 (11th Cir. 1998) (§ 1981); Harrison v. Eddy Potash, Inc., 112 F.3d 1437, 1453 (10th Cir. 1997) (Title VII); Brisentine v. Stone & Webster Engg. Corp., 117 F.3d 519, 526 (11th Cir. 1997) (ADA); Penny v. United Parcel Serv., 128 F.3d 408, 414 (6th Cir. 1997) (ADA); Varner v. National Super Markets, 94 F.3d 1209, 1213 (8th Cir. 1996) (Title VII); Tran v. Tran, 54 F.3d 115, 117 (2d Cir. 1995) (FLSA). The Supreme Court recently granted certiorari to resolve this question, but ultimately decided in Wright v. Universal Maritime Serv. Corp., 119 S. Ct. 391 (1998), only that a collective bargaining agreement's general arbitration clause was not an express or knowing and voluntary waiver; thus, arbitration was not required. *Wright*, therefore, left open the underlying question of whether a properly drafted collective bargaining agreement could terminate a union member's right to sue in federal court on her Title VII claims. See also Doyle v. Raley's Inc, 158 F.3d 1012 (9th Cir. 1998) (because the terms of a collective bargaining agreement between a union and an employer did not indicate that statutory claims were included within the scope of an arbitration clause, an employee's age and disability claims were not arbitrable).

Outside the collective bargaining context, the possible significance of *Gilmer* for rights under Title VII and other antidiscrimination statutes is immense. *Gilmer* clearly applies to Title VII and other antidiscrimination statutes. Seus v. Nuveen, 146 F.3d 175 (3d Cir. 1998) (Title VII and ADEA); McWilliams v. Logicon, Inc., 143 F.3d 573 (10th Cir. 1998) (ADA); Paladino v. Avnet Computer Techs., Inc., 134 F.3d 1054 (11th Cir. 1998) (Title VII);

Miller v. Public Storage Management, Inc., 121 F.3d 215 (5th Cir. 1997) (ADA); Patterson v. Tenet Healthcare, Inc., 113 F.3d 832 (8th Cir. 1997) (Title VII). Because arbitration was a condition of plaintiff's employment in *Gilmer*, companies wishing to avoid suit might require all employees to sign an arbitration agreement. The effect would be to limit any statutory or common law claims to an arbitral forum, which, at best, might be expected to be less sympathetic to employees with respect to remedies. Some believe that arbitrators might be more inclined toward employers on liability issues than would a jury in federal court. One reason is the "repeat player" phenomenon. The EEOC maintains that mandatory arbitration has a built-in bias favoring employers who tend to be "repeat players." This bias may be even stronger when the employer is making use of a repeat arbitrator. See generally Lisa B. Bingham, On Repeat Players, Adhesive Contracts, and the Use of Statistics in Judicial Review of Employment Arbitration Awards, 29 McGeorge L. Rev. 223 (1998). Possible bias of arbitrators is subject to review under the Federal Arbitration Act, but only in extreme cases. A court may not overturn an arbitrator's decision merely because it believes that the arbitrator is wrong on the facts or the law. The FAA provides an award may be vacated where it was procured by corruption, fraud, or undue means, there was evident partiality or corruption in the arbitrators' decision, the arbitrators were guilty of misconduct, or they exceeded their powers. 9 U.S.C.A. §10(a) (1998). While this is a very narrow scope of review, the courts have also held that an award may be vacated when there has been a manifest disregard for the law. Halligan v. Piper Jaffray, Inc., 148 F.3d 197, (2d Cir. 1998).

Some commentators and courts, however, have sought to limit *Gilmer*. The arbitration agreement there was a part of plaintiff's registration with the New York Stock Exchange, not directly a contract with the brokerage firm that employed him. For that reason, the *Gilmer* Court did not address a claim that the Federal Arbitration Act did not apply. Section 1 of the FAA provides that "nothing herein contained shall apply to contracts of employment of seamen, railroad employees, or any other class of workers engaged in foreign or interstate commerce." Arguably, the Court could deprive *Gilmer* of much practical effect by reading this to exclude coverage of all employment contracts, and one circuit has so held. Craft v. Campbell Soup Company, 161 F.3d 1199 (9th Cir. 1998) (FAA is not applicable to individual employment contracts or collective bargaining agreements since they do not fall within the ordinary concept of a contract "evidencing a transaction"). See generally Samuel Estreicher, Predispute Agreements to Arbitrate Statutory Employment Claims, 72 N.Y.U. L. Rev. 1344 (1997); Jeffrey W. Stempel, Reconsidering the Employment Contract Exclusion in Section 1 of the Federal Arbitration Act: Correcting the Judiciary's Failure of Statutory Vision, 1991 J. Dis. Res. 259; Maria C. Whittaker, Gilmer v. Interstate: Liberal Policy Favoring Arbitration Trammels Policy Against Employment Discrimination, 56 Alb. L. Rev. 273 (1992). Such a broad reading of the § 1 exclusion seems unlikely, however, for two reasons. First, the more natural reading of this language is that it excludes collective bargaining agreements — contracts with "classes of workers." Secondly, the majority of courts construe the FAA exclusion narrowly to reach only those workers directly engaged in the transportation of interstate or foreign commerce. See, e.g., Miller v. Logicon, Inc., 143 F.3d 573 (10th Cir. 1998); Cole v. Burns, 105 F.3d 1465 (D.C. Cir. 1997); Miller v. Public Storage, 121 F.3d 215 (5th Cir. 1997); Harrison v. Eddy, 112 F.3d 1437 (10th Cir. 1997); Great Western Mortgage Corp. v. Michele, 110 F.3d 222 (3d Cir. 1997); Patterson v. Tenet Healthcare, 113 F.3d 832 (8th Cir. 1997); Rojas v. TK Communications, Inc., 87 F.3d 745 (5th Cir. 1996). In any event, excluding an arbitration agreement from the FAA does not necessarily invalidate it. Such clauses may still be enforceable, even in federal court, under state arbitration laws or state common law.

The Civil Rights Act of 1991, while not addressing *Gilmer* directly, added a clause to Title VII that has been argued both to fortify and to preclude the use of arbitration agreements required as a condition of employment. Section 118 of the statute provides: "Where appropriate and to the extent authorized by law, the use of alternative means of dispute resolution, including settlement negotiations, conciliation, facilitation, mediation, fact-finding, minitrials, and arbitration, is encouraged to resolve disputes arising under the Acts or provisions of Federal law amended by this title." On its face, the statute is redundant: it "encourages" only alternative dispute resolution that is already "authorized by law." Strictly read, therefore, it does not bear on the question of the proper interpretation of the FAA. Nor is the legislative history helpful: the Section-by-Section Analysis of the Administration refers approvingly to *Gilmer*, 137 Cong. Rec. S15,478 (daily ed. Oct. 30, 1991), while the House Committee Report emphasized that "any agreement to submit disputed issues to arbitration, whether in the context of a collective bargaining agreement or in an employment contract, does not preclude the affected person from seeking relief under the enforcement provisions of Title VII." H.R. Rep. No. 40, 102d Cong., 1st Sess., pt. 1, at 97 (1991). See generally Douglas E. Abrams, Arbitrability in Recent Federal Civil Rights Legislation: The Need for Amendment, 26 Conn. L. Rev. 521 (1994) (arguing that the texts of the ADA and the 1991 Civil Rights Act, "the only sources assured of judicial effectuation," favor enforcing arbitration agreements, even if the legislative histories "acknowledge qualifications on the binding effect arbitral awards would otherwise hold under the FAA").

Section 118 was recently utilized by the court in Duffield v. Robertson Stephens & Co., 144 F.3d 1182 (9th Cir.), *cert. denied,* 119 S. Ct. 95 (1998), to limit arbitration. The Ninth Circuit held that the Civil Rights Act of 1991 prohibits employers from requiring their employees, as a condition of employment, to waive their right to bring future Title VII. Cole v. Burns, 105 F.3d 1465 (D.C. Cir. 1997) also holds that an employer may not condition employment on acceptance of arbitration agreement that requires employee to submit his or her statutory claims to arbitration. See also Pryner v. Tractor Supply Co., 109 F.3d 354 (7th Cir. 1997). But see Seus v. Nuveen, 146 F.3d 175 (3d Cir. 1998).

The problem ultimately is not whether alternative dispute resolution is appropriate to resolve discrimination cases: it is universally agreed that alternative techniques such as arbitration are frequently superior. Rather, the issue is when the parties should be taken to have agreed to replace traditional methods of adjudication with arbitration. See Nelson v. Cyprus Bagdad Copper Corp., 119 F.3d 756 (9th Cir. 1997) (arbitration clause in employment handbook not enforceable even though employee acknowledged its receipt and agreed to read and understand its content). The critics of *Gilmer* are concerned that employees would be required to agree to arbitrate their discrimination claims as a condition of employment, a possibility the *Gilmer* Court downplayed. Some subsequent decisions, however, have upheld such conditions. E.g., Borg-Warner Protective Servs. Corp. v. Gottlieb, 116 F.3d 1485 (9th Cir. 1997) (mandatory arbitration agreement, signed as a condition of employment, does not constitute economic duress or coercion, and thus is enforceable). See generally Stephen J. Ware, Employment Arbitration and Voluntary Consent, 25 Hofstra L. Rev. 83 (1996) (ensuring voluntary consent to arbitration agreements, even those required as a condition of employment, can be attained by employing the contract law doctrines of mutual assent and duress).

Ironically, another development may mean that *Gilmer*, although arising under the ADEA, is good law for all discrimination statutes other than the ADEA under which it was decided. The Older Workers Benefit Protection Act (OWBPA), Pub. L. No. 101-521, 104 Stat. 978 (Oct. 16, 1990) (codified at 29 U.S.C.A. §626 (f)), while not speaking expressly of "arbitration," requires any waiver of ADEA "rights and claims" to be "knowing and voluntary." If this includes the waiver of procedural rights such as a jury trial, the OWBPA may invalidate many agreements to arbitrate that are exacted mechanically as a condition of employment. See generally Christine Godsil Cooper, Where Are We Going with *Gilmer?* — Some Ruminations on the Arbitration of Discrimination Claims, 11 St. Louis U. Pub. L. Rev. 203, 235-236 (1992). Contra Rosenberg v. Merrill Lynch, 163 F.3d 53 (1st Cir. 1998); Seus v. Nuveen, 146 F.3d 175 (3d Cir. 1998) (rejecting claim that, since the language "any right or claim" must encompass the right to a jury trial, OWBPA prohibits the enforcement of any agreement that requires the individual to forgo her statutory right). Williams v. Cigna Financial Advisors, Inc., 56 F.3d 656 (5th Cir. 1995) (OWBPA is inapplicable to arbitration agreements). See also Douglas E. Abrams, Arbitrability in Recent Federal Civil Rights Legislation: The Need for Amendment, 26 Conn. L. Rev. 521, 556 n.187 (1994) (arguing that "Congress did not intend the OWBPA's waiver provision to affect the FAA mandate's operation with respect to either post-dispute or predispute arbitration agreements"). The Supreme Court's recent decision in *Oubre*, see

p. 99 of this Supplement, while not addressing these issues directly, applied OWBPA literally.

Of course, even if arbitration agreements entered into by individual employees are generally enforceable, the courts must still determine whether a particular agreement is valid and whether the arbitration clause reaches the dispute in question. Courts have struggled with whether general language in an arbitration agreement includes employment discrimination claims. Some courts seem hostile to the notion, holding that the employee must have "knowingly" agreed to arbitrate such claims and this requirement is not satisfied unless the agreement clearly refers to employment discrimination claims. E.g., Paladino v. Avnet Computer, 134 F.3d 1054 (11th Cir. 1998) (to fall within the FAA, an arbitration agreement must contain terms that generally and fairly inform the signatories that it covers statutory claims although it need not list every statute); Brisintine v. Stone & Webster Engineering, 117 F.3d 519 (11th Cir. 1997) (agreement must authorize arbitrator to resolve federal statutory claims rather than merely authorizing arbitrator to resolve contract claims); Prudential Ins. Co. v. Lai, 42 F.3d 1299 (9th Cir. 1994). Farrand v. Lutheran Broth., 993 F.2d 1253 (7th Cir. 1993). See also Wright v. Universal Maritime Serv. Corp, 119 S. Ct. 391 (1998) (for a union to waive employees' rights to a federal judicial forum for statutory antidiscrimination claims, the agreement to arbitrate such claims must be clear and unmistakable; a clause providing only for arbitration of "[m]atters under dispute," without explicit incorporation of statutory antidiscrimination requirements is not sufficient); Renteria v. Prudential Ins. Co., 113 F.3d 1104 (9th Cir. 1997) (a U-4 form, stating that arbitrable disputes encompass those "as amended from time to time", was ineffective as a waiver since a knowing waiver of a right must be determined at the time the agreement is made); Shankle v. B-G Maintenance, 163 F.3d 1230 (10th Cir. 1999) (arbitration agreement entered into as a condition of employment which requires the employee to pay a portion of the arbitrator's fees is unenforceable under the FAA; to supplant a judicial forum, arbitration must provide an effective and accessible forum, and the prohibitive cost the employee would have been required to pay meant that the arbitral forum was not accessible); Rosenberg v. Merrill Lynch, 163 F.3d 53 (1st Cir. 1998) (arbitration agreement not enforceable because employer did not explain the range of claims covered by the agreement or provide arbitration rules); Kresock v. Bankers Trust Co., 21 F.3d 176 (7th Cir. 1994) (amendment to agreement not retroactive without consent). See generally Joseph R. Grodin, Arbitration of Employment Discrimination Claims: Doctrine and Policy in the Wake of Gilmer, 14 Hofstra Lab. L.J. 1 (1996). However, more than one court has held that general language includes discrimination claims. Seus v. Nuveen, 146 F.3d 175 (3d Cir. 1998) (rejecting a heightened knowing and voluntary standard that considers such factors as specificity of language in agreement, plaintiff's education and experience, plaintiff's opportunity for deliberation and negotiation, and whether plaintiff was encouraged to consult counsel); Rojas v. TK Communications, Inc., 87 F.3d 745 (5th Cir. 1996); Kidd v. Equitable Life Assurance Socy., 32 F.3d 516 (11th Cir. 1994); Bender v. A.G. Edwards & Sons, Inc., 971 F.2d 698 (11th Cir. 1992). See also Patterson v. Tenet Healthcare, 113 F.3d 832 (8th Cir. 1997) (general language of arbitration clause in employee handbook encompassed federal statutory claims even though other portions of handbook disclaimed contractual obligation).

Whatever the ultimate federal rules, the states cannot alter the scheme created by the FAA and other federal laws. The Supreme Court has reiterated that state laws requiring special treatment of arbitration clauses are pre-empted by the Federal Arbitration Act. Doctors Assocs., Inc. v. Casarotto, 517 U.S. 681 (1996). See also Southland Corp. v. Keating, 465 U.S. 1 (1984) (in enacting the FAA, Congress declared "a national policy favoring arbitration" and "withdrew the power of the states to require a judicial forum for the resolution of claims which the contracting parties agreed to resolve by arbitration"). See generally Traci L. Jones, State Law of Contract Formation in the Shadow of the Federal Arbitration Act, 46 Duke L.J. 653 (1996). While state law principles applicable to contracts generally are, in effect, incorporated into the FAA on its own terms, that statute precludes states from singling out agreements to arbitrate for special treatment. Compare Stirlen v. Supercuts, Inc., 60 Cal. Rptr. 2d 138 (Ct. App. 1997) (arbitration agreement unenforceable on the basis of unconscionability, a neutral principle applicable to contracts generally).

Page 1114.   Add after second sentence in second full paragraph:

See Rao v. County of Fairfax, Va., 108 F.3d 42 (4th Cir. 1997) (unfavorable state agency decision does not preclude subsequent Title VII suit, even though agency decision was adjudicatory and would have been given binding effect in state court).

Page 1116.   Add after third paragraph:

Assuming preclusion principles are applicable, the court must pay close attention to the requirements for preclusion. E.g., Pleming v. Universal-Rundle Corp., 142 F.3d 1354 (11th Cir. 1998) (res judicata did not bar current claims based on two hiring decisions occurring after filing of prior claim, even though, in course of prior litigation, parties briefed and discussed incidents giving rise to second suit); Rivers v. Barbeton Bd. of Educ., 143 F.3d 1029 (6th Cir. 1998) (res judicata barred an employee's second race discrimination claim because she erroneously delayed litigating her original claim by not obtaining a right-to-sue latter during a 15-month pendency of the action)

D.   PRIVATE ENFORCEMENT: RELATIONSHIP OF THE EEOC CHARGE TO PRIVATE SUIT

1.   *Proper Plaintiffs*

Page 1122.   Add at end of carryover paragraph:

But see Childress v. City of Richmond, Virginia, 134 F.3d 1205, 1209 (4th Cir. 1998) (to qualify as an "aggrieved person" under Title VII, the plaintiff must be a member of the class of direct victims of conduct prohibited by Title VII; thus, white male police officers did not have standing to bring a claim regarding their immediate supervisor's derogatory remarks to and about female and African American police officers).

E.   PRIVATE CLASS ACTIONS

2.   *Requirements of Rule 23(a)*

Page 1142.   Add new Note 14A:

14A. A recent amendment to FRCP 23 regarding class actions, effective December 1, 1998, adds a new paragraph:

> (f) Appeals. A court of appeals may in its discretion permit an appeal from an order of a district court granting or denying class action certification under this rule if application is made to it within ten days after entry of the order. An appeal does not stay proceedings in the district court unless the district judge or the court of appeals so orders.

Will the possibility of interlocutory appeal encourage or discourage class actions?

3.   *Requirements of Rule 23(b)*

Page 1144.   Add at end of second full paragraph:

E.g. Allison v. Citgo Petroleum Corp., 151 F.3d 402 (5th Cir. 1998) (2-1) (upholding district court determination that suit seeking compensatory and punitive damages could not be certified under (b)(2) because such relief was not incidental to the declarative and injunctive relief sought).

Page 1145.   Insert after Wetzel *cite in first line after first block quote:*

See generally George Rutherglen, Better Late Than Never: Notice and Opt-Out at the Settlement Stage of Class Actions, 71 N.Y.U. L. Rev. 258 (1996); George Rutherglen, Notice, Scope and Preclusion in the Title VII Class Actions, 69 Va. L. Rev. 11 (1983). The suggestion that individual members of a proper (b)(2) class do not have a right to opt out of the class has, in fact, been held explicitly. Kyriazi v. Western Elec. Co., 647 F.2d 388 (3d Cir. 1981). See also Eubanks v. Billington, 110 F.3d 87 (D.C. Cir. 1997) (while class members do not have an unqualified right to opt-out, district courts may accord such rights as part of their power to manage the class action); Thompson v. Albright 139 F.3d 227 (D.C. Cir. 1997) (permitting class members to opt out was an abuse of discretion since the right to opt out of a non-(b)(3) action is not expressly provided in Rule 23(c)(2) and the district court did not adduce any tenable ground upon which opting out might be permitted).

Page 1146.   Add after first full paragraph:

Recently, the Supreme Court upheld a decertification of a 23 (b)(3) "settlement only" class. See Amchem Prods. v. Windsor, 521 U.S. 591 (1997). This decision could have far reaching effects, conceivably limiting, if not extinguishing, the viability of discrimination class actions. While *Amchem* arose under tort law, specifically asbestos litigation, the opinion's delineation of the problems and conflicts of the class there mirror problems that are frequently present in employment discrimination class actions.

In *Amchem*, the purported class was compromised of two distinct groups of plaintiffs, those with current injuries and those with exposure-only claims. The Supreme Court found numerous conflicts of interest among these two groups as well as numerous differing issues and claims requiring resolution. As a result, the requirement of Rule 23(b)(3) that common questions of law or fact predominate over any questions affecting only individual members was not satisfied. Further, Rule 23 (a)(4)'s adequacy of representation requirement was not met.

The Supreme Court noted several distinguishing features of the class at issue that accounted for its holding. First, *Amchem* involved different states' tort laws, which varied widely on available causes of action. Second, the class was certified under 23(b)(3) in which class cohesiveness is not as evident nor aggregation as clearly called for as in 23(b)(1) and 23(b)(2) actions. Third, because *Amchem* involved claims asserting personal injury and death, the individual plaintiffs had a significant interest in controlling the prosecution of their cases. The Court noted that mass accident cases are not "ordinarily appropriate" for class treatment when the stakes are high and the disparities among the individual class members are great. Fourth, the class was certified as a settlement class which, the Supreme Court stated, may deserve heightened scrutiny because of the lack of opportunity to adjust the class as the case unfolds. Finally, the Court found that the named plaintiffs, all of whom had current injuries, could not adequately represent the interests of exposure-only plaintiffs, who were not similarly situated.

While these distinctions may temper the effect of *Amchem's* holding in the employment area, it is too early to predict the impact of this case. An employment discrimination class action, for instance, could, to a large degree, comfortably fit within these same parameters, e.g., a class action in a disparate impact context, seeking monetary as well as injunctive relief. In such a scenario, most of the concerns that the Supreme Court expressed in *Amchem* would be present. For example, the individual claims for back pay would undercut the cohesiveness of the class, making it resemble a 23(b)(3) action, whether or not it was certified as such. Money damages could run high, which in turn would create a significant interest for the plaintiffs to individually control their case. Also, the impact of such discrimination may vary widely among these individual plaintiffs. Further, if the named plaintiffs were current employees and the class encompassed other groups (e.g., discharged employees and applicants), adequacy of representation would be questionable. Conflicts among these varied class members could also exist.

4. The Preclusive Effects of a Class Action

Page 1148.   Insert in last paragraph after id. cite:

See also Basch v. Ground Round, 139 F.3d 6 (1st Cir. 1998) (holding that stacking of two sequential class claims was improper basis for tolling statute of limitations on ADEA claims under *Crown, Cork*).

F. FEDERAL GOVERNMENT ENFORCEMENT

Page 1152.   Add after carryover paragraph:

There have also been efforts to limit EEOC suits on behalf of individual employers. While no one questions that double recovery ought to be avoided, a recent decision effectively prevented the EEOC from suing for monetary relief when the employees in question have waived their rights to a judicial forum by agreeing to arbitration. EEOC v. Kidder, Peabody & Co. 156 F.3d 298 (2d Cir. 1998) (EEOC may not pursue monetary relief in an age discrimination case on behalf of securities industry employees who signed an arbitration agreement).

G. THE RELATIONSHIP BETWEEN PUBLIC AND PRIVATE SUIT

Page 1156. *Add in carryover paragraph after citation to* **McClure:**

But see Paolito v. John Brown E. & C. Inc. 151 F. 3d 60 (2d Cir. 1998) (findings of EEOC or equivalent state agencies are not required, as a matter of law, to be admitted in subsequent trials of employment discrimination actions, inasmuch as the probative value of such findings does not necessarily outweigh any danger of unfair prejudice). EEOC v. Ford Motor Co., 98 F.3d 1341 (6th Cir. 1996) (although admission is within the discretion of the district court, there was no error in a court's categorical refusal to admit EEOC cause determinations in either bench or jury trials.)

Page 1156. *Add at end of carryover paragraph:*

Michael D. Moberly, Reconsidering the Impact of Reasonable Cause Determinations in the Ninth Circuit, 24 Pepperdine L. Rev. 37 (1996) (criticizing the Ninth Circuit for not only establishing a rule of per se admissibility but also for holding that a reasonable cause determination is a per se basis to deny summary judgment to a defendant).

H. TITLE VII SUIT AGAINST GOVERNMENTAL EMPLOYERS

Page 1156. *Delete last sentence in last full paragraph and insert:*

Statutes, like Title VII, which are valid exercises of Congress' power under § 5 of the 14th Amendment will trump state sovereignty under the Eleventh Amendment although the statutes must not only be valid under § 5 but also unequivocally express an intent to override the states' Eleventh Amendment immunity. Seminole Tribe of Florida v. Florida, 517 U.S. 44 (1996). That case also held that the commerce clause is not a valid basis for abrogating state Eleventh Amendment immunity. Thus, at a minimum, *Seminole Tribe* prevents federal court enforcement of the ADEA and ADA against entities that count as the state under that Amendment unless such statutes can be justified by Congress' power under § 5 of the 14th Amendment and Congress indicates clearly enough that it intends to override the states' Eleventh Amendment immunity. In that regard, City of Boerne v. Flores, 521 U.S. 507 (1997), while limited to striking down the Religious Freedom Restoration Act as it applied to state and local governments, suggests a more searching review of enactments under § 5 than was previously true.

While the Supreme Court has explicitly held that Title VII suits against the states in federal court are permitted, Fitzpatrick v. Bitzer, 447 U.S. 425 (1976), it has not yet decided whether this is true of the ADA or ADEA. However, the Supreme Court has recently granted certiorari in Kimel v. Florida Bd. of Regents, 139 F.3d 1426 (11th Cir. 1998), cert. granted, 119 S. Ct. 901 (1999), a case in which the Eleventh Circuit found that Congress did not unmistakably indicate an intent to abrogate states' Eleventh Amendment immunity from ADEA suits in federal court. To this point, there is a split in the circuits regarding ADEA claims against states in federal court, although most have held that such suits are valid. *Compare* Migneualt v. Peck, 158 F.2d 1131 (10th Cir. 1998) (Eleventh Amendment does not immunize University of New Mexico from a former employee's ADEA suit); Hurd v. Pittsburg State University, 109 F.3d 1540 (10th Cir. 1997) (same); Keeton v. University of Nevada Sys., 150 F.3d 1055 (9th Cir. 1998) (same); Coger v. Tennessee Bd. of Regents, 154 F.3d 296 (6th Cir. 1998) (same) *with* Humenansky v. Regents of University of Minnesota, 152 F.3d 822 (8th Cir. 1998) (Congress did not express a clear intent to abrogate Eleventh Amendment immunity under the ADEA and, furthermore, the ADEA was not a valid exercise of power under § 5 of the Fourteenth Amendment); Kimel v. Florida Bd. of Regents, 139 F.3d 1426 (11th Cir. 1998), 119 S. Ct. 901 (1999) (Congress did not unmistakably indicate an intent to abrogate states' Eleventh Amendment immunity concerning the ADEA). As to the ADA, the authority is much sparser. See *Kimel v. Florida Bd. of Regents, supra* (ADA claim was valid since Congress abrogated states' Eleventh Amendment immunity in suits under the ADA). See also Autio v. AFSCME, Local 3139, 140 F.3d 802 (8th Cir. 1998) (6-6 en banc decision affirms district court determination that ADA claims against state not barred by the Eleventh Amendment). See generally, Note, Elizabeth Welter, The ADA's Abrogation of Eleventh Amendment State Immunity as a Valid Exercise of Congress's Power to Enforce the Fourteenth Amendment, 82 Minn. L. Rev. 1139 (1998); Note, Edward P. Noonan, the ADEA in the Wake of *Seminole*, 31 U. Rich. L. Rev. 879 (1997).

I.   SETTLING DISCRIMINATION SUITS

Page 1173.   Insert in Note 4 after second sentence:

When such parties are joined, or successfully intervene, their rights must be adjudicated, and cannot be altered by the agreement of the original parties. See United States v. City of Hialeah, 140 F.3d 968 (11th Cir. 1998) (2-1) (intervenor who objects to a decree cannot have its rights modified without its consent).

Chapter 11

Judicial Relief

B. RELIEF FOR INDIVIDUAL DISCRIMINATION

1. Backpay

Page 1193.   Replace last two sentences in Note 5 with:

With respect to Eleventh Amendment limitations on ADEA and ADA suits, see Supplement p. 163.

Page 1194.   Add after second sentence in Note 6:

Interest should not be denied simply because the discriminatee violated his or her duty to mitigate damages, Booker v. Taylor Milk Co., 64 F.3d 860 (3d Cir. 1995), but can be denied when the discriminatee has recovered sufficient damages to make him or her whole. Criado v. IBM Corp., 145 F.3d 437 (1st Cir. 1998).

3. Frontpay

Page 1205. Add at end of Note 5:

But see Ramirez v. New York City Off-Track Betting Corp., 112 F.3d 38 (2d Cir. 1997).

Page 1205. Add new Note 7:

7. In Padilla v. Metro-North Commuter R.R., 92 F.3d 117 (2d Cir. 1996), *cert. denied*, 117 S. Ct. 2453 (1997), an employee demoted in violation of the ADEA was denied reinstatement, but was awarded continuing front pay for his reduction in future salary (about $20,000 per year) until he either left the company or retired (in about 25 years). The appellate court upheld the award, noting that reinstatement was infeasible due to animosity and the employee had no reasonable prospect of obtaining comparable employment. Won't this award lead to additional animosity and litigation?

4. Compensatory and Punitive Damages

Page 1206. Add at the end of the third full paragraph:

The Sixth Circuit recently held that the statutory caps apply on a "per plaintiff, per lawsuit" basis, not a "per claim" basis. Thus, a discriminatee who prevails on multiple claims and receives both compensatory and punitive damages on each claim has her overall recovery of damages limited to the amount of the cap. Hudson v. Reno, 130 F.3d 1193 (6th Cir. 1997), *cert. denied*, 119 S.Ct. 64 (1998).

Page 1206. At the end of the fourth full paragraph, add footnote callout "***" and accompanying footnote at bottom of page:

***Despite the apparent clarity of § 1981a(b), the courts are split on whether a front pay award is included in applying the statutory cap. See Kramer v. Logan Cty. Sch. Dist., 157 F.3d 620 (8th Cir. 1998), and the cases cited there.

Page 1207. Add after second full paragraph:

Contra, Ferguson v. City of Phoenix, 157 F.3d 668 (9th Cir. 1998) (without citing *Smith*).

The prediction that courts will have "no difficulty" in construing Title II of the ADA to allow the recovery of compensatory damages for intentional disability discrimination may be doubtful after the Supreme Court's 5-4 decision in Gebser v. Lago Vista Ind. Sch. Dist., 118 S. Ct. 1989 (1998). *Gebser* was a sexual harassment suit by a student under Title IX of the Education Amendments of 1972, 20 U.S.C.A. § 1681, which prohibits sex discrimination in federally-funded education programs. The Court held that compensatory damages can be recovered from the school district only where the discrimination results from the school district's official policy or the school district "has actual notice of, and is deliberately indifferent to, the teacher's misconduct." 118 S. Ct. at 1991. The dissenters objected to imposing this prerequisite to the recovery of compensatory damages.

Title II, like Title IX, is based on the enforcement scheme for Title VI of the Civil Rights Act of 1964, 42 U.S.C.A. § 2000d, which prohibits race, color, and national origin discrimination in federally-funded programs. See 42 U.S.C.A. § 12133 and 29 U.S.C.A. § 794a. Thus *Gebser* may be applicable in Title II actions. On the other hand, the legislative history of Title II states that Congress intended to create a private right of action with the "full panoply of available remedies," H. Rep. No. 485 (III), 101st Cong., 2d Sess. 52 (1990), *reprinted in* 1990 U.S.C.C.A.N. 445, 475, which arguably precludes the *Gebser* limitation.

A later Sixth Circuit decision held that compensatory damages are available for intentional discrimination in violation of Title II without referring to *Gebser*. Johnson v. City of Saline, 151 F.3d 564 (6th Cir. 1998).

Page 1207.   *Add at end of first sentence in third full paragraph before period:*

, Johnson v. City of Saline, 151 F.3d 564 (6th Cir. 1998).

Page 1211.   *Add at end of Note 1:*

However, several courts have set aside awards for mental distress when the discriminatee presented only his own testimony, especially when his testimony established nothing more than hurt feelings, anger, frustration, embarrassment, and disappointment. See Patterson v. P.H.P. Healthcare Corp., 90 F.3d 927 (5th Cir. 1996), *cert. denied*, 519 U.S. 1091 (1997); Price v. City of Charlotte, 93 F.3d 1241 (4th Cir. 1996), and the cases discussed there.

Page 1212.   *Add at end of Note 2:*

In Williams v. Pharmacia, Inc., 137 F.3d 944 (7th Cir. 1998), the court held that a Title VII plaintiff can recover both compensatory damages for lost future earning capacity and a front pay award. The jury found that the discharged plaintiff had experienced sex discrimination and unlawful retaliation and awarded her $300,000 in compensatory damages, including $250,000 for lost future earnings. The judge then added $180,000 for lost backpay and denying reinstatement, another $115,530 for one year's front pay. The appellate court held that the plaintiff's poor job evaluations and termination justified the jury's award of damages for lost future earning capacity. The front pay award compensated a different injury — the loss plaintiff suffered from her failure to regain her old job. Do you find this reasoning convincing? Didn't the jury's award compensate the plaintiff for lost earnings for the first year in which she wouldn't have had any? Would a different result have been reached if the front pay award had been based on losses to the date of retirement?

Page 1212.   Add at end of Note 3:

The Supreme Court relied in part on the avoidable consequences doctrine in formulating the affirmative defense set forth in *Ellerth,* Supplement p. 63. Why did the Court say that this defense applies to "liability *or damages*" (italics added)? Is it possible for the defense to fail as to liability but prevail as to damages?

Page 1212.   Add at end of Note 4:

In Deffenbaugh-Williams v. Wal-Mart Stores, Inc., 156 F.3d 581 (5th Cir. 1998), the court held that §§1981 and 1981a impose vicarious liability for punitive damages on the employer where a supervisor discriminates with respect to a tangible employment action, such as discharge or demotion, regardless of the employer's knowledge or conduct. The court relied on the Supreme Court's decision in *Ellerth,* Supplement p. 63. Is this the implication of that precedents?

Page 1212.   Add at end of Note 5:

Most circuits think the "malice or reckless indifference" standard for punitive damages requires a showing of wrongful intent beyond the discriminatory intent necessary to establish liability. E.g., Browning v. President Riverboat Casino-Mo., Inc., 139 F.3d 631 (8th Cir. 1998); Ngo v. Reno Hilton Resort Corp., 156 F.3d 988 (9th Cir. 1998); Kolstad v. American Dental Assn., 108 F.3d 1431 (D.C. Cir. 1998) (en banc), *cert. granted,* 119 S. Ct. 401 (1998). There are some recent decisions to the contrary, Criado v. IBM Corp., 145

B. Relief for Individual Discrimination

F.3d 437 (1st Cir. 1998); Merriweather v. Family Dollar Stores, Inc., 103 F.3d 576 (7th Cir. 1996), but these decisions seem inconsistent with other recent decisions from the same circuits. E.g., Tincher v. Wal-Mart Stores, Inc., 118 F.3d 1125 (7th Cir. 1997); McKennon v. Kwong Wah Restaurant, 83 F.3d 498 (1st Cir. 1996). In any event, the Supreme Court should resolve the issue with its decision in *Kolstad.*

Page 1215. Add at end of first full paragraph:

The Tenth Circuit backed away from this dicta in Haynes v. Williams, 88 F.3d 898 (10th Cir. 1996). See also Lissa v. Southern Food Serv., Inc., 159 F.3d 177 (4th Cir. 1998), and Huckabay v. Moore, 142 F.3d 233 (5th Cir. 1998).

6. Attorneys' Fees

Page 1227. Add to Note 2 after the "E.g." in the second line:

Saski v. Class, 92 F.3d 232 (4th Cir. 1996) ("generous award" of damages received);

Page 1229. Add new Note 9:

9. Title VII contains a special fee provision which is applicable only in certain mixed-motives cases, § 706(g)(2)(B)(i), 42 U.S.C.A. § 2000e-5(g)(2)(B)(i). When the plaintiff has shown the employer used an unlawful factor in making a decision, but the employer shows that it would have made the same decision even if the unlawful factor had not been used, the court "may grant" attorney's fees to the plaintiff. The decision to make a fee award under this provision turns on such factors as whether the plaintiff has obtained injunctive or declaratory relief, the public interest in the litigation, and the conduct of the parties. Canup v. Chipman-Union, Inc., 123 F.3d 1440 (11th Cir. 1997); Sheppard v. Riverview Nursing Ctr., Inc., 88 F.3d 1332 (4th Cir.), *cert. denied,* 519 U.S. 993 (1996). But see Gudenkauf v. Staffer Communications, Inc., 158 F.3d 1074 (10th Cir. 1998). Thus, the standards for making a fee award under § 706(k) are inapplicable, although the rules for calculating the amount of the award should be the same. If the defendant prevails in a mixed-motives case, the defendant's eligibility for a fee award is governed by § 706(k). Akrabawi v. Carnes Co., 152 F.3d 688 (7th Cir. 1998).

7. Lack of Causation as a Remedial Limitation

*Page 1231.   Add after second comma in footnote "**":*

see Provencher v. CVS Pharmacy Div. of Melville Corp., 145 F.3d 5 (1st Cir. 1998),

*Page 1231.   Add at end of footnote "**":*

Contra, Allison v. Citgo Petro. Corp., 151 F.3d 402 (5th Cir. 1998).

Page 1232.   Add after "See also" in first line of text:

Price v. City of Charlotte, 93 F.3d 1241 (4th Cir. 1996);

Page 1232.   Add at end of second line:

But see Schultz v. YMCA, 139 F.3d 286 (1st Cir. 1998).

C.   RELIEF FOR SYSTEMIC DISCRIMINATION

1.   Retroactive Seniority and Backpay

Page 1244.   Add before last sentence in Note 3:

See also Taxman v. Board of Educ., 91 F.3d 1547 (3d Cir. 1996), *cert. dismissed,* 118 S. Ct. 595 (1997).

D.   CALCULATION OF BACKPAY

2.   The Duty to Mitigate Damages

Page 1276.   Add at end of first full paragraph:

D. Calculation of Backpay

However, a recent decision from the Second Circuit followed *Weaver* by holding that the employer established the failure to mitigate by showing that the plaintiff failed to make a reasonable effort to find comparable employment. Moreover, the plaintiff, by failing to mitigate, was ineligible for a front pay award. Greenway v. Buffalo Hilton Hotel, 143 F.3d 47 (2d Cir. 1998).

Page 1282.   Add at end of Note 4:

Another court has explained that, where the plaintiff has failed to exhaust in-house remedies before resigning, the court may conclude that the employee did not consider the working conditions intolerable. Lindale v. Tokheim Corp., 145 F.3d 953 (7th Cir. 1998). Is this explanation convincing?